SUFFER THE CAPTIVE CHILDREN

From Industrial School to Reluctant Exile

by

Steve Joyce

Note for Librarians: a cataloguing record for this book that includes Dewey Classification and US Library of Congress numbers is available from the National Library of Canada. The complete cataloguing record can be obtained from the National Library's online database at:
www.nlc-bnc.ca/amicus/index-e.html
ISBN 1-4120-2084-0

TRAFFORD

This book was published on-demand in cooperation with Trafford Publishing. On-demand publishing is a unique process and service of making a book available for retail sale to the public taking advantage of on-demand manufacturing and Internet marketing. On-demand publishing includes promotions, retail sales, manufacturing, order fulfilment, accounting and collecting royalties on behalf of the author.

Suite 6E, 2333 Government St., Victoria, B.C. V8T 4P4, CANADA
Phone 250-383-6864   Toll-free 1-888-232-4444 (Canada & US)
Fax 250-383-6804   E-mail sales@trafford.com   Web site www.trafford.com
TRAFFORD PUBLISHING IS A DIVISION OF TRAFFORD HOLDINGS LTD.
Trafford Catalogue #04-0008   www.trafford.com/robots/04-0008.html

10   9   8   7   6   5   4   3   2

ACKNOWLEDGEMENTS

I want to thank my wife, Rita and my sons John, Tim and Terry for helping me to relive my youth, which I thought lost forever.

CONTENTS

ABOUT THE AUTHOR

Steve Joyce was born in Recess in the Joyce Country of Connemara in County Galway. At the age of three his father's work took the family to Tuam in north Galway where he attended the local schools. At the age of eleven tragedy struck which inspired him to write this book.

He left Ireland at the age of twenty and now lives in Manchester in England with his wife. They have three sons, two close to the family home and the eldest in West Sussex. Their sons have made a success of their lives, and there are seven grandchildren.

From his infancy in Connemara, through the tragic deaths of his mother and sister within six months, to his cruel treatment at the hands of the Christian Brothers, in spite of many sad happenings the author recalls lots of humorous events connected with his work, and his involvement in the sports of Gaelic football, rugby, soccer, golf, and boxing, at which he became a champion, and went on to a successful career as coach to a club in Manchester. He was also appointed team manager and trainer of the Manchester and Lancashire boys' boxing teams.

CHAPTER 1

In the Beginning

It all began for me in the lovely village of Lissoughter, in the townland of Recess, Connemara in County Galway. My father had adopted the role of breadwinner for a family of four boys and two girls, when his father died at an early age. It was an awesome responsibility for a young lad, but he was determined to do everything in his power to help his mother out. He had to sacrifice his own chance of a proper schooling, but he made sure that the rest of the family never missed a day off school. They were always grateful to him, even though they thought him a hard taskmaster, and too strict at times.

It was a difficult time to bring up a family in Ireland, as the country was engaged in a bitter struggle for independence against a foreign army of occupation. The Irish people had been engaged off and on for seven hundred years in trying to get rid of the British, but now they also had the hated *Black and Tans*[1] rampaging through the country. The 'Tans' as they were called by the Irish people, were seen by the local populace as a lawless band of thugs who killed, raped and plundered

---

[1] *Black and Tans*, a recruited band comprised mostly of ex World War One soldiers and, it has been said, released criminals so named because of twin coloured uniform.

everywhere they went, and seemed to meet with no word of disapproval from the British government of the time.

This was the country my father was trying to raise his family in, so it is not difficult to understand why he was so strict. His family, though they lived in a fairly remote part of the country, did not escape the attention of the Tans. They were at their fireside saying the rosary one evening when they heard a *Crossley Tender*[2] coming up the narrow lane in front of my grandmother's thatched cottage, and they knew right away that it was the hated Tans. The door was kicked in by half a dozen drunken louts in Tan uniforms and they broke every piece of furniture in the house. They tore a picture of *Robert Emmet*[3] from over the mantelpiece and they threw it into the fire. That band of warriors then lined up the family at gunpoint, and debated on what to do with the "Fenian bastards" as they called them. One hero suggested that they shoot them all, but my grandmother pleaded with them not to kill her family. Her plea seemed to touch some hidden spark of decency in the drink-sodden brain of the yob in charge, and he shouted at them to leave. He then shouted that they had some serious drinking to do, and after firing a volley of shots in the air they drove off, singing 'There is no flag afloat like the Union Jack.' I

---

[2] *Crossley Tender* – a troop carrier built in Manchester used by Black and Tans.
[3] *Robert Emmet* – Irish Patriot executed by British in Thomas Street, Dublin in 1803.

wonder where the term *'Butchers Apron'*[4] came from. They were not as heroic some time later when they encountered *Tom Barry's*[5] Column at *Kilmichael*[6]. It is amazing what a few glasses of Irish whiskey can do. Their serious drinking later proved an expensive one for the people of Clifden. When they had had their fill of drink they set a few shops on fire, and fired a few shots at the railway workmen whom they missed, (probably because they were all drunk,) and sang 'Rule Britannia' to the people who were struggling to put out the fires. The officer in charge then shouted 'Send the bill to Michael Collins', as they drove away. The people lived in fear of those savages and their evil deeds will never be forgotten, though they have long departed from our shores. I have often heard it said by people who lived through those awful times that the Tans were the dregs of the slums of England, and in many instances released convicts. True or false Lloyd George told them to make our country a hell for rebels to live in, and if they failed to do so it was not for want of trying.

The Future Foretold

My father's brothers were now fine strapping young men contributing their share of work on the farm, and my father had time for an occasional drink with his friends.

---

[4] **Butchers' Apron** – Name given to Union Flag by the Irish.
[5] **Tom Barry** – Most successful IRA Leader in Anglo Irish War from 1919 to 1921.
[6] **Kilmichael** – Ambush by Flying Column led by Tom Barry resulted in death of 17 Black and Tans in West Cork.

He was in his own mind, and in the eyes of the family, a confirmed bachelor, as he never had time in his youth to meet members of the opposite sex. I often heard my father relate the story of how a foal was stolen from his stables and he was determined to catch the thief. Meeting with no success he visited a fortune teller in Clifden, who it was said was gifted with uncanny powers and second sight. When he visited this lady she just told him to sit down across the room facing her. She frowned and said 'you are better off not knowing who stole the animal, as you would end up doing something you would regret.' She went on to tell him that he would be getting married soon, and that he had better forget the foal. My father laughed and said that he was well past the age for getting married, and told her that she did not know what she was talking about. She just smiled and said 'you will have a different story to tell in six months' time.'

He left her complaining bitterly of fortune tellers who knew nothing and were taking money by false pretence. She had also mentioned that his future wife was on board a ship sailing for Ireland, and this further convinced him that she was a phoney. The only girl he had been friendly with had gone to America some time before, and he had not heard that she was returning home. It came to pass however as he was talking to some friends after mass that he came face to face with my mother, newly arrived from America. My mother was already called Joyce as that part of west Galway is called Joyce Country on the map of Ireland, so I can rightly claim to be a true Joyce. They arranged to meet again, and soon found that their friendship had grown into love, and to the surprise of everyone the bachelor in his middle forties was planning to wed. They were married in the parish of Roundstone some three months later by an old friend of my father, a Father Gleeson, and decided that their future lay in America. Ireland had little to offer its people at that time, as it struggled to recover from the Anglo Irish war of independence, and the bitter Civil War that followed it, which often saw brothers fighting on opposite sides.

As Strong as a Horse

It was just as well that the fortune teller had not named the horse thief as my father who was as strong as a horse could be a bad man to cross, and to the present day older people speak of his feats of strength. Normally he was a gentle giant, but I believe he could be very difficult if he had been drinking when old grievances, real or imagined, would come to mind. One Sunday after mass he visited a shebeen with a few pals to drink potheen, and returning home later he got into an argument with two members of The Royal Irish Constabulary. They told him to go home if he knew what was good for him - he then told them to go home to a place with a much warmer climate. When they tried to arrest him, two very wet R. I. C. men had to be fished out of the lake, and when he finally got home there were six of the same gentlemen waiting at his mother's house and they asked him to accompany them to the R. I. C. station. He was well tanked up with potheen and more than ready for

5

battle no matter what the odds, but his mother begged him not to cause any trouble so off he went.

When they got to the station the Inspector, a good sport knowing dad's reputation said, "if you put the gloves on with the R. I. C. heavyweight champion, we will not prefer any charges". He was given black coffee and time to sober up, and then all hell broke loose. My father who had never had a glove on in his life was taking a terrible beating, but he kept swinging and missing, and as the big sergeant tired he landed a mighty haymaker and nearly dislocated the champions` neck. His head hit the window shutter snapping off the top hinge, and I am told it remained so until the demise of the RIC. He then wrestled him to the ground, placed his knee on his neck, and would have killed him had they not pulled him off. My dad had clearly never heard of the Marquis of Queensbury, but the Inspector asked him to join the force and they would teach him to box, and told him he could go a long way. I am afraid he asked the wrong man, as my father hated everything they stood for.

My cousin told me that two officers helped dad home once when he was drunk, and he showed his gratitude by banging their heads together when they got as far as my grandmother's house - he did not like the R. I. C. I was with my father many years later, and a very large older man hailed him from the other side of the street, "Are you Sean Mor (big John)" he enquired, and when dad replied "yes", he said "I want to buy you a drink". My father broke his lifelong pledge that evening, and

6

drank with an ex R. I. C. man. He was the ex champion sergeant, and two old men got pleasantly drunk together, and old grievances were forgotten, My father in his younger days would never have been seen in their company.

Boston or Tuam?

The Free State government had agreed, under duress, to pay the retirement pensions of the Royal Irish Constabulary, now disbanded, made up almost entirely of renegade Irishmen, who sold their souls for foreign gold. They were very mannerly and always raised their hats when greeting the few people who spoke to them, but the Irish are slow to forget, and they had been the eyes and ears of the Army of occupation. They are all dead now and not missed - they were hated and detested by the majority of the people, and the country is better off without them. It is easy now, with the Celtic Tiger the talk of Europe, for the revisionists to be critical of the people who were running our country then, but the only money available to the government then was the National Loan organised by the now dead *Michael Collins*[7], and whatever was given by our many good friends in America. Seven hundred years of foreign occupation and absentee landlords had bled the country dry, and the people who were trying to right the many wrongs were the freedom fighters of yesterday, who had no experience to call on. I can well understand why my

---

[7] ***Michael Collins*** – Irish Republican Army Leader killed in West Cork in August 1922 in Irish Civil War.

parents wanted to emigrate, and it was agreed that my mother, now pregnant with my sister who was to die tragically at an early age, would go to her sister who lived in Boston, and my father would follow when he had tidied up his affairs at home.

At the thought of losing her oldest son for ever my grandmother got more depressed daily, as my mother, now in Boston, was looking for a place to make a home for the family. Prior to my mother's departure for America, my father had applied for a job on the railway, more in hope than confidence, as it was almost impossible to get work at that time. He did not know whether to laugh or cry when the offer of a job arrived in the post. The depressed state of his mother helped him to decide. My mother never wanted to leave Ireland in the first place, so he gratefully accepted the job and wrote telling her to return. It was winter and the baby was almost due, so they agreed to delay her return until after the baby was born. My sister arrived on Christmas day 1930, and two months later my mother sailed for Ireland to be greeted in Galway by my overjoyed father, and they returned to Connemara planning to build a new house and spend the rest of their lives there.

They lost no time in getting started; having put every penny they had into their new home. There was no shortage of helpers, as his brothers (now big able men) were willing to give the builder every assistance. The chosen site was on one of the nicest spots in the village, with beautiful views of the surrounding mountains and the little river flowing through the valley below. In my mind's eye I can still see the stepping stones through the shallow water making a short cut to the rough track (now a tarred road). The river has been diverted, and it all looks different now. The building sand was quarried from the riverbed, and the rest of the building materials were ordered from Corbetts in Galway, a company still in business today.

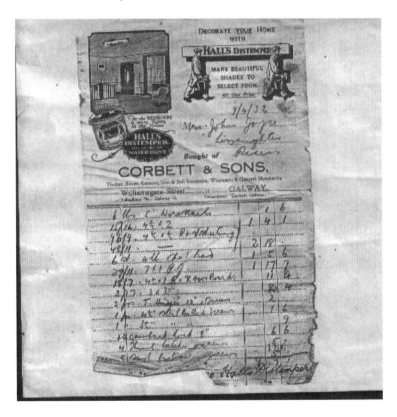

There was great celebrating the day they moved in with what furniture they could afford, and planning to add to it when things got better. Their joy was short lived however, as the rumour spread that the railway was going to close down. No one believed it at first, but their worst fears were realised when they were notified in writing that the Galway to Clifden line would be closing down a month from the following week. Despair spread through the area when they heard the awful news, as the railway was the only means of employment available to the men of the district.

The threat of emigration loomed, and this of course meant the breaking up of families, as the men would have to leave in search of work. Some of them owned land, as did my father, but it was of poor quality and only fit to graze sheep and could not provide a decent standard of living for a family. My parents were at their wits' end not knowing what to do, as I had appeared on the scene two years after my mother's return from the States, to be followed by my brother John eighteen months later. There was deep gloom in the village when the rails were lifted and loaded on the last train ever to leave Recess station. My father was approached by the *permanent way inspector*[8], a man who did not mix much with his workmen, on the day the station closed. He said "I can offer you a job John, but it would mean moving your family to a town forty miles from here". He added

---

[8] **Permanent Way Inspector** – The man in charge of the maintenance staff on the railroad (plate layers, drivers, firemen, etc.)

"You are a good worker and a house would be provided. Think about it and talk it over with your wife, I need to know your answer by next week."

If my parents could see what the future held in store for the family, I think they might have stayed in Connemara and hoped for the best. Were the Galway to Clifden line in existence today it would be a major tourist attraction, but the government of that time was busily engaged in cost cutting exercises, with the economy in a perilous state. My parents decided to accept the offer, and we moved to the town of Tuam in north Galway. I still remember with sadness the tears streaming down my grandmother's face as we said our farewells. We were only moving forty miles, but to her we were leaving forever. People tend to forget that at that time very few people owned a car, and only the shopkeepers and the wealthy folk enjoyed the luxury of having their own transport. Certainly no one on my father's income could afford the like. For many years afterwards we would spend our summer holidays with my grandmother in her lovely thatched cottage - happy days.

At that time American wakes were common. They were a kind of farewell party for the departing immigrant, and I believe they were very sad affairs. The parents said goodbye to their children, knowing that they would never see them again. Another custom I witnessed in Connemara that I did not like was listening to the caoners or keeners as they are called in English, when my maternal grandmother died. They kept up this awful

Banshee-like wailing at the wake, and as children it scared us half to death, I saw a similar performance at a Jewish funeral years later, and it brought it all back. I can only say that it adds to peoples' grief.

We arrived in Tuam, and I can remember even to this day the wonder of my father opening the door and switching on the electric light. It is easy to understand the effect this had on a child not yet four years old, who had never known anything but an oil lamp in a farmhouse. It seemed pure magic. The immediate neighbours soon became good friends, and those of them still living remain good friends today. Life settled down in our new home, and we started to make friends of the neighbours' children. Though many long years have passed since then, I can recall how strange it felt going out to play in the mornings with our new friends. Even at that early age, I felt homesick for the peace and tranquillity of Connemara, the mountains and the little river that flowed past our home. I also missed the trips on my uncle Joe's shoulders to fish for trout, and I can in my mind's eye see the fish, their bellies flashing in the sunlight as he threw them onto the bank. He was gifted at the art of tickling trout, something I have seen attempted many times since, but without much success. I can also recall my uncle Joe asking me not to tell my dad when a cow knocked me down when I was about three years old. My uncle was looking after me at the time and knowing dad's temper did not want to upset him. He need not have worried. I loved my uncle and I would never betray him, and forty years later we were talking about the old days and he mentioned it. It was still fresh in our memories after all those years.

CHAPTER 2

Starting School

Convent School

One Sunday a couple of ladies in long black habits called to our house. I was playing with a little boy from next door at the time, and I was frightened of them, as I had no idea who they were. My pal said, "The nuns are here". I soon found out that they always called at houses where there were young children of school age. The Mercy Convent nuns visited again the following Sunday, when it was arranged that my sister would start school. When Monday arrived my mother, accompanied by my brother and myself took Mary to the Convent, and arranged to call for her at three o'clock. From then on it became my mother's daily routine, rain or shine, to make the double journey. It was not long before the ladies in black decided that it was my turn to start school, and a very frightened four-year-old said a tearful goodbye to his mother and young brother at the Convent. For a moment I thought my mother was crying also, but she explained that a fly had gone into her eye, which was strange as it was raining at the time.

I well recall my first day at school, from the moment the nun told my mother, "You had better go, Mrs Joyce, Stephen will be fine." I was told to sit at a table with

14

other children, and I was given a piece of chalk and blackboard to play with. I decided that I liked school, and we were given milk and biscuits later on. I needed to go to the toilet badly and I desperately tried to hold on until my mother arrived, and I hoped she would soon call for me. I suddenly realised that I had wet my pants, and I started to cry. I found out that morning what the strap on the desk was for. When my mother arrived to take me home, on seeing my tear stained face, asked me what was wrong. Sister Peter said that I had been a very naughty boy, and my legs were slapped for the second time that day. I decided then that school was not a nice place. I can see the foxy faced Sister Peter with her piggy eyes, who caused me and indeed a lot of other children sleepless nights, and also in my mind's eye her partner in crime, one Sister Joseph. Those two little vixens put the fear of God into terrified little children, when a kind word would have made the world and school a much brighter place. I wonder why they chose mens' names. Could it be that there was something missing from their lives?

The one redeeming feature of my first year at school was the time spent in the care of saintly old Mother Dominic, a gentle old soul who broke my heart when she died. I doubt if any hearts broke when the other two departed this mortal plane. On looking back now, it seems to me that a cruel streak seemed to be part and parcel of the requirement to enter the teaching profession in Ireland at that time. I count among my friends many English people who tell me the teachers they feared and hated most were the Irish teachers at their schools. When I collect my grandchildren from school and see their cheerful laughing faces, I thank God that they are enjoying their schooldays and don't have to suffer the sadists we encountered.

In a changed world I am sure the parents of today would never tolerate such behaviour. I blame the clergy for not stamping on the sadists who hid behind their religious garb. They were not blind to what was going on, but I am sad to say that at that time they formed a mutual admiration society with the nuns. My brother followed me to the Convent of Mercy, but we rarely talked about school as we learned to accept regular punishment as a normal procedure.

My sister Mary became something of a celebrity when she was awarded the faine, a gold ring worn on the person to symbolise the fact that the wearer was fluent in the Irish language. Speaking our native Gaelic language came easy to Connemara natives then, as it was spoken in almost every home west of the river Corrib. My parents always spoke Irish in the home, and I heard it more often than English from my cradle days. The rosary was always said in Irish in our home by my father, and we responded in the same tongue, a lovely habit that sadly seems to have died out over the years, but I am afraid the Ireland of today differs from those days in many ways. The Gaelic as spoken in the schools was always referred to by my father as 'book Irish', not to be confused with the Irish he had learned from the cradle, and in Tuam it was rarely spoken outside the classroom. It was strange that the old town had strayed from its roots, and Irish was rarely spoken in the town, despite the fact that the natives of the district fought valiantly against the murderous Black and Tans, who burned it to the ground. I came to regard Tuam as my hometown, and while I refer to myself as a Connemara man, when people ask me where I come from, having grown up there I say Tuam. I still love it even though some of the most painful memories of my boyhood are associated with the old town, and I am nearly a stranger there now, though a few of my old pals still live there.

The Christian Brothers' School

I am afraid I am allowing myself to stray away from my Convent days. It was the custom (and indeed it probably still is), for boys on reaching the age of seven to move up to the *Christian Brothers school*[9] on the Dublin road. Having made my first Communion before leaving the Convent, I was ready for my great adventure. We started at the Brothers in Mr Murphy's class, and were delighted to find that the horror stories told to us by the older boys were without foundation, they were just told to put the fear of God into us. They told of savage beatings dished out by the male teachers, and having suffered at the hands of the nuns, we were easily convinced. Mr Murphy was a jolly man known as 'Spud' to the boys, and as well as being a really good teacher, he was a well-

---

[9] **CBS (ChristianBrothers Schools)** – The Order was founded by Brother Ignatius Rice in Waterford in 1803.

respected local historian. He told us of the awful suffering of our people in the famine years₈, and of the coffin ships that sailed from Cobh, often arriving in America with less than half the number they started out with. He told us about how our land was taken from us by the invader, and how our people rebelled down the centuries, refusing to submit to the invader. This made us proud of being Irish and he instilled in all a love of our homeland; that has remained with me all my life, and indeed I will carry it with me to my grave. There were no beatings, no violence - just a lovely atmosphere in Mr Murphy's classroom, and he told us that the ancient town of Tuam was once the Capital of Ireland and the seat of King Turlough O'Connor the High King of Ireland.

It was unbelievable the happiness that lovely man generated and we broke up for the summer holidays in happy mood, and eagerly looking forward to the year ahead. This was a complete contrast to the sickening feeling of unhappiness and dread we experienced, when the Priest announced at Mass, "The Christian Brothers school, the Mercy Convent, and Presentation schools will reopen tomorrow," during our years in the Convent. I must confess though before I move on from the subject of the nuns, that the vast majority of nuns were good kind people who exuded goodness and kindness. My family will always be indebted to Saintly Sister Aloysius, who nursed my mother some time later when sickness came to our home, and indeed was there at her bedside to recite the prayers for the dying as she passed peacefully away. I always try to think of that good nun, when my mind goes back to the cruel little tyrants who took delight in the suffering of little children.

Our year in Mr Murphy's class passed too quickly, and we felt very grown up as we filed into Mr Quinn's classroom to be greeted by the big man. Paddy Quinn as he was called was a giant of a man who taught us to sing our National Anthem, and many other patriotic ballads now rarely if ever sung in Ireland, and it appears to me that today's young people seem to find it distasteful to mention the savage treatment meted out to our people over the centuries. It is indeed strange that you can attend a concert in any part of England, and hear all our ballads sung, often by English people. The Wolfe Tones tour regularly and play to packed halls, and you can buy their records in any town in England. I for one count among my friends many English people, and in fairness I can only say that they are real friends whom I believe I could rely on totally. I find them decent people who bear us no animosity, and indeed I can only describe them as a fair-minded people. In my early years in Britain I saw adverts on lodging houses that read 'No Dogs No Blacks No Irish'. This at a time when British agents were busy travelling all over our country trying to recruit Irish doctors, nurses and tradesmen, to come over and help to rebuild their war-ravaged country. At that time there were a few left who thought they still ruled the world, and I truly believe that a minority think so still. They are to be seen regularly attacking people at football matches at home and abroad, and they seem to take delight in wrecking property, inflicting hurt on total strangers, and singing offensive songs. They bring shame on their country, and on decent English people everywhere. The same people would no doubt call other people terrorists for trying to reclaim what is rightfully theirs. It would appear that there is in their minds, one law for them and another for the rest of us. I truly believe that the politicians are greatly to blame for a lot of the problems that have plagued the Irish people through the centuries, as soldiers are trained to obey orders, and I know the German war criminals tried that one in Nuremberg without success, but am sure regular soldiers do as they are ordered (the murderous Black and Tans being an exception.) Paddy Quinn told us that we should always stand up for what we believed in, and I am sure he was right.

Paddy was a keen sportsman and encouraged us to play our native games, hurling and Gaelic football. He gave freely of his time to help the boys in his care, and he also took an active interest in the running of the boxing and athletic clubs. He had a tendency to dwell a lot on the political happenings in our country, without trying to influence us in the direction of any particular party. I mention this as I feel that it would be difficult, if not impossible, to explain things as they were in Ireland then without doing so. There were three lay teachers on the staff of the Christian Brothers school at that time, but circumstances forced my brother and me to leave before I reached the sixth standard, which was taught by Paddy Noon. Those friends of mine who benefited from his teaching had nothing but good to say about him. When we moved up to Brother Mcaulif's class he seemed to concentrate more on the educational side than the political, but I feel I must stress that nearly all the Christian Brothers were fiercely nationalist, in fact now as I look back to that era, I am convinced that they were instructed to teach us to lean that way also. Brother Mac as we called him was a far- sighted man and a wonderful teacher. He taught us decimals, and the metric system, and tried to impress on us the belief that we would see a united Europe one day. He also said that he was certain that man would one day walk on the Moon, which amused us all. This great teacher was far ahead of his time, and I am sure his talents were wasted on the likes of us. I often wonder what became of him, and I am afraid scant attention was paid to his metric system. I feel his time would have been of more benefit to College students, where I feel he was well qualified to teach. Though I feel we all learned a lot from Brother Mac, I have often thought of our year in his class as a year of wasted opportunities. If only we had paid better attention, we could have learned much more.

Before we moved on to Brother Vaughan's class, Mac called us to attention. He told us to always walk tall, and to try to adopt a soldierly bearing. He was a man who certainly practised what he preached. He said that if you do not respect yourself no one else would. He then shook every boy in the class by the hand and wished us luck in our future lives.

CHAPTER 3

Life Gets Harder

Death Strikes our House

That day as we broke up for the summer holidays, I never dreamed that shortly my life would change forever. My mother complained one evening of a pain in her side, and my father made her take a cup of hot milk and go to bed early. He saw no reason to send for the doctor, and said she would be better in the morning. When morning came the pain was worse and my father sent for the doctor. When he had examined my mother he called my father to one side, and spoke in a whisper and said, "I will deal with it right away John." My sister and young brother and I went to school as usual thinking there was nothing wrong. When we got home from school that evening we were told by our next door neighbour that our mother had been taken to the hospital for a check up. She assured us that there was nothing to worry about and that she would be home in a day or two. My mother did come home a few days later and I heard her tell my sister Mary that they had put her in the T B ward. I was very angry on hearing this and I said to my Dad they should not have put my Mum in the T B ward, as she only had a cold. I was not to know then that mother would shortly take to her bed and remain there until she died.

During the early forties tuberculosis was a death sentence and only spoken of in whispers in Ireland. My mother carried on as normal for a few weeks but she seemed to tire very easily, something that had never happened as far as I could remember in the past. I came in from play one evening and I was very upset when I saw both parents in tears. My mother was clutching a blood stained hand towel and I then saw her cough up blood. For the first time I was terrified. I can only imagine how my poor parents must have felt. My mother finally took to her bed as winter drew near, and but for a brief period at Christmas when she attempted to help my sister prepare the dinner, she never left it until her death. My father continued to go to work every day, and though he was without doubt the strongest man I ever met, I still do not understand how he kept going, getting little or no sleep. Only someone who has watched a loved one dying a bit more every day can imagine how my father suffered during this awful time. My mother got thinner by the day and her face turned a strange bright red, her eyes sunk deep into her face as she continued to cough up her lifeblood. We were discouraged from going in to her room to visit her by my father and by Sister Aloysius, a kindly nun who spent every minute she could spare as an unpaid nurse. Now that I am older and wiser I know they were afraid we would catch the killer T. B. We arrived home from school on a cold February evening and were given our dinner by a neighbour, who then told us our mother had died. I cannot describe the awful gloom that descended on our home at that time as my poor father struggled with the household chores, doing the cooking for the evening meal and washing clothes as best he could. We buried my mother on a dark dismal February day, and returning home afterwards no one uttered a word, as we all tried to deal with our own personal heart break.

My father must have been distraught as he pondered on what to do as he wondered what was to become of his young family. He contacted some family members and enquired about the possibility of us going to live with them until he could decide what to do. The position was desperate as far as he was concerned, as it was evident that things could not continue as they were at present. The response from the family was a great disappointment to my dad, as no one refused outright to help him but they could only take one of us. This would mean that each of us would be separated, and to Dad it only seemed to make things worse, not better. He thought it over as he tried to carry on doing all he could to run the home. I can now understand why his family were reluctant to risk the possibility of the dreaded killer disease being brought into their homes, and while I fully sympathise with their position, I can also understand why Dad felt badly let down. He had sacrificed his youth to rear his family, and there was no help available to him in his hour of need. His problems got even worse when my sister Mary was confined to bed with a bad cold, and when it persisted the doctor sent her to the Galway hospital to be examined. The awful news was broken to Dad by our doctor. Mary was being detained in the T. B. ward in the Galway hospital. The good doctor said that hopefully they had caught her in time, and the ward doctor assured him that she stood a good chance of a full recovery.

Fate Steps In

To say that things were as bad as they could possibly get would be an accurate description of our situation at this awful time. It was of vital importance if my brother and I were to escape the same fate that we would have to go to live somewhere else - but where? My father was desperate and did not know which way to turn as he explained his situation to his boss on the railway. He was a big Kerry man, who had given my dad every possible help during my mother's illness, and suggested that an enquiry should be made about the possibility of a place being found for us in Saint Joseph's school in Galway. It was explained to my father by his boss Mr Keane that St Joseph's was a school for orphans and deprived children, and that it was being run by the good Christian Brothers so we would be in good hands if we were fortunate enough to be accepted.

I was now in Brother Vaughan's class in Tuam, and I had enjoyed my time in the Brothers school much more than I had my time with the nuns, so the prospect of going to Galway did not seem too bad. Given a choice of course I would have stayed at home, but I knew that could not be. Brother Vaughan was a County Limerick man who loved the game of hurling and proudly displayed the Mackey Brothers pictures on the classroom wall. The Mackeys at that time were the best known hurlers in Ireland, and they of course also came from Limerick. I was happy in his class, and only for the way things were at home I would never have asked to leave it. My pals told me later on that they had really enjoyed their year in Vaughan's class. This was not to be for myself however and Galway and St Joseph's was where I was to spend the next four years of my young life. My dad told my brother and me that the good Christian Brothers had kindly offered to take us in, and that the Railway Benevolent Society, of which he was a member, had arranged it for us. Little did the poor man realise what he was sentencing his young sons to.

My father, as I explained earlier, had only a basic education and he placed an awful amount of trust in others, and on this occasion it led to an awful lot of suffering for my brother and me. Not for one moment would I suggest that there was anything dishonest about Mr Keane, and I am certain that he meant well, but I do believe that if his own children were involved he would have done a bit more research into St Joseph's, or San Quentin as we came to know it. With a heavy heart Dad prepared for our departure by fitting us out with complete new clothing for our big adventure, spending money he could ill afford, presumably in the hope of improving relations with 'the good Christian Brothers' as Mr Keane liked to call them. Brother Vaughan came to my desk one day in class and said, "I hear you are going to Galway". I answered "Yes sir", and he said "It is a fine school and I know you will be happy there." He then told me that he often called there and that he would call to see us in the future. I did in fact see him there on one occasion but I expect he had long forgotten that I existed.

Leaving Home

The day finally arrived for us to say goodbye to the Christian Brothers School in Tuam, and my eyes filled up with tears when Brother Vaughan asked the class to stand and pray that myself and my brother would be happy in our new school. As I left the classroom every one of the boys shook my hand and said, "Good luck Stephen". I was too full up to talk, as John and I made our way home. My father was full of false gaiety as he went about preparing a meal for us, on what was to be our last evening at home for a long time. The neighbours called to say goodbye and some of them brought little gifts for my brother and me. It was time for bed and I noticed that Dad's eyes filled up as he kissed us good night. I awoke from a troubled sleep in answer to Dads call, "It's time to get up boys, we must not miss the Galway bus." We got on the bus at Tuam railway station and soon we were on our way.

When we arrived in Galway there was a large Christian Brother waiting to meet us. He had wavy fair hair, and he gave us very little time to say goodbye to Dad which I think was just as well, as I am certain that it would have been too painful for all three of us. He assured our father that we would be fine and said there was no need to worry as we were in good hands. Dad stood waving goodbye to us as we walked along with Brother Ryan through Eyre Square, and he was no sooner out of sight than Ryan jumped on his bicycle and we had to run to keep up with him. He said it was not far to the College, and I suppose it was only about three miles, but for an eleven year old and a nine year old it was hard work running to keep up with a bicycle, as we carried our few belongings in parcels under our arms. It was the one and only time I heard it called a college. Ryan certainly had a sense of humour that was not at all funny.

St Joseph's Industrial School

When we arrived at St Joseph's we were taken to the kitchen where we were given bread and butter and tea, and then released into the large school yard, where we were surrounded by a curious crowd of poorly dressed boys. A few started to ask us questions, but they were soon moved on when a large Brother started slapping their faces left and right as he shouted at them to clear off. He then warned my brother and me that we had better behave ourselves if we wanted to stay out of trouble.

This then was my introduction to St Joseph's college and the brutal Brother Langan. I was called in to the big assembly hall a little later by Brother Ryan, and he told me to go to the top floor with my brother and wait for him. I had to enquire how to get there, as it was all strange to me. I was directed there by a man whom I thought was a teacher, and he had only one arm. I found out later that he was the night watchman, and his name was John Judge. Ryan was waiting there for us and he said, "Follow me". He took us into what I thought must be the biggest bedroom in the world, pointed to a bed and said "Stephen you will sleep here". He again said, "Follow me" and took us to the other end of the room where he pointed to a bed and said, "This is your bed, John". I said, "Excuse me sir, but my father asked you if we could sleep near each other and you said you would arrange it." I was not prepared for what happened next. Without warning I received a stinging slap across the face from Ryan's hand, and he said "You are not in Tuam now and you will obey orders or we may have to teach you discipline." I started to cry and I said, "I will tell my dad", but this made Ryan even angrier and he shouted "Your dad cannot hear you, and you are here because he could not control you."

"Entrance Certificate?"

I cried myself to sleep that night, and determined that I would write home next day and tell Dad what Ryan had done. I was awakened early next morning by shouts and someone banging on the beds saying "Get up and get washed." I followed the other boys into the next room and saw a long line of wash basins in a line. I started to wash myself in the icy cold water when I was confronted by Brother Langan and he shouted "Joyce where is your towel?" No one had told me my towel was on my bed and I had not brought it with me. I was sent to collect it with a clout across the head. The rest of the boys hurriedly made their beds and rushed from the dormitory over to another room with rows of pews and an altar, where a priest was starting to say Mass. I was the last to arrive and I had difficulty in finding a seat. I saw my young brother and he looked near to tears.

When the Mass ended we all headed for the refectory, as they called the place, where we ate breakfast. We were each given a plate of dripping and two slices of dry bread. We were then given a mug of tea with a rounded rim, where the congested food from meals long eaten had congealed. I was not thirsty. I politely asked Ryan if I could write home and he said I could, and added, "Don't seal it until I have read it." I had, in spite of my youth shown great wisdom when I said to Dad the day we left home "If we are unhappy I will ask in my letter if Ann Delaney has started school yet," (Ann was the little girl next door.) I did ask the question but I am afraid poor Dad had more pressing things on his mind as my sister Mary got weaker by the day. When class finished for the day, Ryan asked me to hand over the letter I had written to my father. He said he would deduct the price of the stamp from my money. He had taken what little funds my brother and I possessed on our arrival, saying that he would keep it safe for us.

We were given a written test to determine which class they should put us in. I was told that I would be in Brother O'Malley's class, and on the first morning I took a seat about five rows from the front of the class after a boy told me there was no one sitting there. I had just taken my seat when O'Malley walked in. He said, "Who told you to sit there? You sit here in the front row where I can keep an eye on you." From that moment on I could do nothing right for Brother O'Malley. He found fault with every thing I did and seemed to hate me.

My brother and I were allowed to visit our sister in the Hospital, and we were shocked to see how much weight she had lost. Her bones seemed to almost come through her skin. Dad called to see us at the end of the month and took us out to the town, where he bought lemonade and cakes for us. He asked us if the Brothers were good to us and we said, "Yes." He seemed so unhappy that we could not tell him the truth. His visit soon ended and it was back to 'San Quentin'. It would be another month before we would see Dad again. The day we arrived Ryan took our new suits and said he would look after them, and we were given old worn clothes that were crawling in vermin. When Sunday arrived we were told to get ready to go for a walk, and I asked Brother Ryan if we could have our new suits. His reply was a slap across the face and he called me an ungrateful boy. We never saw our new clothes again.

CHAPTER 4

What did I do?

The walk seemed to go on forever as we marched in fours almost as far as Spidal, a village nearly ten miles from Salthill where St Joseph's was situated. Brother O'Malley led the walk and he seemed tireless. Brother Ryan had assured us all that he was sorry he could not go with us but he had a lot to do. I was told by a boy who worked in the kitchen that Ryan went for a sleep every Sunday afternoon while we were on the walk. We were weak with hunger when we got back to the school and ready for our dinner. Dinner was a watery mess with traces of meat mixed with what looked like the food our neighbour fed to his pigs in Tuam, and a big Christian Brother called Gaynor was in charge of the kitchen and he punished any boy he caught talking. The sight of the slops they called dinner made me feel sick and I pushed it aside, but some of the other lads nearly fought over it and said "You will soon be glad to get it". Sadly I must confess their words came true.

The following day Ryan asked what was my favourite sport and I answered "Football" though I had never seen a football game. He then took me to the large assembly hall and fitted me out with boxing gloves and told me I was to box a boy who was already gloved up. I got the father and mother of a pasting, and as each round ended Ryan asked if I had enough, some stubborn streak in me made me answer "no". I was still there after the three rounds ended but I was black and blue for days and both my eyes were almost closed. I was told later that my opponent was the *Connacht schoolboy champion*[10].

I had by now decided that I did not like Brother Ryan. In fact I did not like O'Malley or Brother Langan either, as they seemed to pick on me for no reason. I wondered why they were so cruel to boys who in many cases were orphans, or from broken homes, and some whose parents did not want them.

We Lose our Sister

We continued to go to visit our sister Mary in the Galway hospital as often as we were allowed, and by now she was totally unrecognisable. If I did not know she was my sister I would have walked past her bed but she always tried to look cheerful, even though we all knew she was dying. We returned to the school from what was to prove the last time we saw Mary, for we were refused admission to see her body or to go to her funeral, despite the fact that a neighbour of ours came to Galway to take us to see her. How my father managed to keep on working or stay sane I will never know, but he never failed to visit us once a month.

---

[10] ***Connacht Schoolboy Champion*** – There are four Provinces in Ireland (Ulster, Munster, Leinster and Connacht).

I was singled out by O'Malley to be regularly punished for no special reason. This bastard seemed to enjoy beating me and passing remarks like "they should not send sick people here, and some people seem to think that this is a T. B. rehabilitation centre". I did not realise at the time because I was too young and innocent, that he was referring to the fact of my mother having died of T. B and my sister having died in Galway hospital of the same disease, and assuming that I too was affected by it. It made sense to me many years later when my wife and I called at St Joseph's and requested a copy of my admission form to the school, which I was reluctantly given. It stated that I was 'T. B. chested'. I thank God that there was no truth in that statement, as I have always enjoyed robust health. He always made nasty remarks about me in front of other boys and I was called T. B. Joyce a few times. I can only assume that he had told some of his favourites about my family's history.

I was often punished by this brute for little or no reason, and on a few occasions as we filed out of the classroom, he would shout "Joyce you were talking in class again". What followed was usually six of the best as he delivered six strokes of a billiard cue, more often than not on the left hand and nearly always on a freezing cold winter's morning. I always tried not to cry but this enraged him and he would shout, "I will break you yet". O'Malley differed from Ryan in that he used a billiard cue, while Ryan used a leather strap made up of two strips of leather stitched together and allegedly reinforced by copper coins, or with his big right hand. The King brute

Langan always used his fist, and he was very proud of his punching power. The secret was to fall down and pretend to be knocked out, as to get up would only be to invite another haymaker. It would be very interesting to see how this animal would have fared against a full-grown man. I for one would have been happy to test him when I was grown to manhood.

I cannot understand even now how so many sadists happened to be thrown together under one roof. It appears to me that being of large build allied to a brutal nature was more important in St Joseph's than an ability to teach. It was so different from the Brothers school in Tuam that I often lay awake at night wondering if this awful nightmare would ever end. It got even worse one night after lights out when I awoke to the sound of a boy screaming, "No more sir please, for Gods sake stop". The beating continued for a long time until the poor unfortunate boy was reduced to pitiful whinging. I thought it was one of the Brothers, but I soon found out it was the night-watchman John Judge who administered corporal punishment nightly, and carried a cane for the purpose. This was the man who had directed me to the dormitory on the day I arrived, and as I mentioned earlier he had only one arm.. I often heard his name whispered by some of the boys, who would stop talking about him if anyone approached them. He ruled the dormitories like one of Hitler's Gestapo, and almost every night some poor lad felt the weight of his one arm. There are hundreds of men who suffered from beatings from this savage who would like to literally disarm him.

Bullying was a common occurrence at the school, and it was this that persuaded me that I should learn to box.

Learning to Box

The school had a thriving boxing class trained on two nights a week by the Irish international bantamweight boxer Sergeant Mick Brennan. He was a fine man who was a renowned boxer and a fine teacher. He hated bullies and he would never tolerate mismatching a boy. He was only half the size of the Brothers who terrorised us but he could handle the biggest of them with ease. I found it difficult enough to defend myself, and I often was called upon to stand up for my young brother, so I joined the boxing class. I vowed to avenge the beating I had received at the hands of the schoolboy champion when I first arrived at St Joseph's, but before I could even set my mind to seek revenge I had a long painful road to travel. I soon outgrew him so it never came to pass, but he was a good lad and we soon became friends. He told me that Ryan had instructed him to give me a good hiding on that occasion, and he did not dare disobey him. It made me hate Ryan all the more. Mr Brennan the trainer told me he could teach me to box, but said it would be a wasted effort if I did not possess an aptitude for the sport. I learned many painful lessons on the way, but the trainer had warned me that there was no short cut or easy way to learn. As time passed I grew big and strong but a bit on the skinny side, but what pleased me most was when Mr Brennan told me I could hold my own with a boy named Buckley who was the head prefect and the Connacht Champion. I also grew to love the noble art.

I was put on boiler house duty with a boy from County Mayo named Dunne. This job was to wheel a truck loaded with logs to the boiler house to feed the furnace. Dunne, who like me had suffered at Ryan's hands, suggested that we should burn his leather strap and I readily agreed and fed it to the furnace with shouts of glee. Ryan soon missed his favourite toy, and the class was not allowed to play football until the culprit was found. Dunne informed on me, and the beatings I had received in the past were as nothing compared to the savage thrashing I suffered on this occasion.

Dunne got some of the treatment traditionally given to informers in County Galway, but first I gave him a lesson that he took some time to recover from. He was ostracised by his classmates from that day. Need I say that our friendship ended there and then. He took the trouble to steer well clear or me from then on, but tried to apologise on one occasion but I ignored him.

The first time I experienced Brother Langan's punching power was when he awoke us from our slumbers by shouting and banging on the beds. This was his usual method and at best he was a bad tempered man. On this particular morning he was in a foul mood, and everyone was extra careful not to invoke the big bully's anger. It was evident that he was in an extra mean condition when he said, "We will have bed inspection this morning so

39

you have been warned." When Langan called an inspection of our beds we were terrified that it would be our unlucky day, as some poor devil always failed to please him and on this occasion it was me. He asked if I was trying to annoy him and I said "No sir", and at that he proceeded to pull the blankets off my bed and he threw them on the floor. I was trembling with fear as he stood and watched me trying to remake the bed and the harder I tried the worse my attempts became and I ended up in tears. He shouted, "You bloody fool" and knocked me down with a punch. I was too frightened to remember to stay down, and as soon as I regained my feet, I received a tremendous punch that left me sprawling at his feet where I remained for some time being unable to rise. I thought my jaw was broken as he walked away, but when I went to see Nurse Hughes later on, she gave me a tablet and said she hoped it would get rid of the pain. She was a very nice lady and she never asked me how I got hurt, as I am sure I was not the first boy Langan had beaten up that she had tried to help, though I thought she looked sorry for me.

This good lady was to become the wife of Mr O`Donnell, one of the three lay teachers on the staff and my favourite teacher. He was a nice man who taught us to play Gaelic football, my favourite sport, and I wondered some years later if he was aware that the Steve Joyce who wore the maroon and white of Galway was his ex pupil- I hope he did.

Regular beatings became part of our daily ritual, and anyone who escaped a beating was indeed fortunate. At times we wondered if there was a God in Heaven. Indeed I often wondered if we would ever get away from 'San Quentin'. The misery continued day after day with no end in sight. It was a harsh cold loveless place. Dickensian would be an apt description. I can still hear the banging on the beds as Langan's harsh voice rang out, and the pathetic cries of one boy named Callaghan who I believe came from Dublin. This unfortunate youth was misshapen in his body and had breasts like a girl. He was constantly beaten and held up to ridicule by both O'Malley and Langan.

It was every boy for himself as the mad rush for the washroom started every morning with fear the spur, and God help any boy who failed to get to the washroom in seconds. We carried our coarse towels with us and they were changed once a week. We handed them in after our weekly bath on Saturday night. Bath night was another occasion when one was lucky to escape without a clout as the pig faced Langan dished out blows to any boy he deemed too slow getting dry and clothed. Naked boys were an easy target for this brutal man. I often wonder now how some boys avoided serious injury or even death, and indeed some boys often seemed to disappear never to be seen again, but no one dared ask where they had gone. To ask a simple question was deemed an impertinence, so we declined to ask if certain boys had left when they disappeared never to be seen by us again.

The good Monks were above reproach. This was clear to be seen when some poor lad would run away after a particularly bad beating and complain to the Gardai (Irish police). They were always returned by the people they had complained to, and received further punishment for running away. In my opinion Ireland has a lot to answer for and in particular the people who turned a blind eye to the way the incarcerated youth of that era were made to suffer, nearly always at the whim of monsters who seemed to enjoy watching children in pain.

I had been told before I was sent to Galway that St Joseph's was a school for orphans and underprivileged children. What a shock I got some time later when I was sent to the home of a policeman to help him to cut his lawn. When he asked what I had done to get sent to an Industrial School, I replied that my mother had died. He then replied "I am sorry to hear that, but you must have committed some misdemeanour to be sent there". From that day to the present, I feel shame every time someone mentions an Industrial School, and I truly believe my brother feels the same. When I returned to the school years later, I started to make enquiries to find out why some of the boys were sent to St Joseph's, and I was shocked to find that most of them had committed some trivial offence like stealing a few apples from an orchard or staying away from school. If the sons of the wealthy had done something similar I feel sure it would be regarded as high spirits, and not something that would send them out into the world in later years burdened with a criminal record, for it was regarded as such. I found out also that some boys were in the same position as myself and my young brother, having lost a parent and in a couple of extreme cases both parents. Regardless of why some unfortunate boys were there, they were treated no better than those who had committed a minor offence .I always felt that Bros Langan and O'Malley, for some unknown reason, had developed a strong dislike for orphaned children like myself, because when there was an unpleasant job to be done one of us always seemed to be picked to do it. I often think that perhaps in their eyes we considered ourselves to be better than the others, but whatever the reason they often enjoyed a laugh at our expense with their cronies who could get away with anything.

I found it rather strange then to find some boys were favoured by Langan in particular more than the rest, but now having seen a lot of strange happenings during my life, I wonder if there was a sinister reason. I never saw certain boys being punished while others were often beaten up for no reason. I certainly feel that I owe a dept to the boxing instructor Mr Brennan because one thing he taught me was to roll with the punches, a priceless asset at St Joseph's. It most certainly helped me to avoid the full force of Langan's fearful right on more than one occasion.

Small Acts of Kindness

There were three lay teachers on the staff at the school - Mr Grenan, Mr Harrington, known as Mocky, and my favourite teacher Mr O'Donnell. They were all three of them very good kind men, who never to my knowledge beat any boy and they were all popular with the boys. I was never fortunate enough to be in their classes, but I got on well with them all. Mocky was a pathetic little man who never seemed to have any money, and often cadged cigarettes from any lad who managed to get some, and Mr Grenan was quite young but prematurely grey. It was said that he immigrated to Canada, and he was never replaced. Mr O'Donnell was a decent human being who made St Josephs a slightly more bearable place for those of us unfortunate enough to be placed at the mercy of the savages in religious habits.

Boys were frequently sent out to work for businessmen in the town, and let it be said that the Brothers only volunteered our services to those who could be of use to them, and they always courted the friendship of the Guards. It is not difficult to see why runaways were always returned to the school promptly and their complaints ignored. If a boy were to be sent out to work he would be inundated with requests to buy comics or sweets by those lucky enough to have a few pence. I was given the task on a few occasions, and I still feel the shame and anger I experienced to feel the shopkeeper's eyes following my every move. It was clear from my shabby dress that I was from the Industrial School, and of course it was assumed by those pillars of society that I had a criminal record.

I often wonder what would have happened if a boy had been injured or killed when out working for people in the town. I feel certain that they were not supposed to send boys out to act as unpaid labourers for shopkeepers and monied people, and if money changed hands we certainly never saw any of it.

CHAPTER 5

Winning and Losing

Mr O'Donnell taught us to play Gaelic football, a game I grew to love, and to my delight I became quite good at it. Mr O'Donnell called a meeting of lads who played football and said " As you all know it has always been my ambition to win the Bishop's Cup for the school, and this year we will make a special effort." The Bishop's Cup was the premier award for Gaelic football in the Galway City schools, and to O'Donnell it was as important as winning the All Ireland final. He held regular training sessions, and when the team was announced I was appointed team captain. The position meant that I handed on Mr O'Donnell's instructions on the field of play, and though in later years I played for the Galway County team, Mr O'Donnell's powers of organisation were the best I ever encountered. If Galway were playing an important game he did a drawing of Croke Park on a large blackboard and filled in the players' names in the colours of the County and the opposition in the same way. It was a small gesture that added to our enjoyment.

To the delight of our trainer and to everyone's surprise, not only did we do well but we remained unbeaten, winning the league easily. The cup was on display on the table in the assembly hall, and all the team members were proud of our success, but my delight was short-lived. It took O'Malley to put a damper on things when he called me over one morning and said, "If you think a game of football changes anything you are sadly mistaken. If you step out of line, I will come down on you like a ton of bricks." This holy monk certainly did everything possible to make my time in captivity, for that was what it was, as miserable as possible. I had some success in avoiding the wrath of "Pig–face" Langan as he was called by all, as Mr O'Donnell decided that he would train an athletics team to try and emulate the footballers' success. It was hard work training on the sands on the shores of Galway Bay, but at least we were well away from the two brutes Langan and O'Malley, who treated us as if we were inferior beings and less than human.

The big day dawned bright and sunny, and Mr O'Donnell and his team were in confident mood as we set out for Saint Mary's College where the sports meeting was held. It was unbelievable what happened, as once more the boys from The 'Indust' as we were known swept all before us, and a second cup went on display. I can only imagine what this did for the good Mr O'Donnell, who really was as much an inmate of that awful place as any of us, and he remained there until he retired some years later. I kept in touch with him until his death a few years ago, and I can only say that the world is a poorer place for his passing as he made life bearable for young boys in that sad place. May he rest in peace.

We were not finished training, as we were told we would be going to Ennistymon in County Clare to challenge the southern winners. When the day came the rain poured from the heavens as we got ready to go, frightened that it would be called off. It went ahead however, and once again we were victorious, and once again I was presented with another cup as captain, our third trophy that year. We continued to compete during the rest of my time at the school but we never reached the heights of that summer of long ago, and never got anywhere near to winning another trophy.

We were now studying hard under Ryan to take our Primary Certificate examination, and he tried to bully knowledge into boys in a short time that they should have been working at all year. He spent most of the time working at English essays, and one was about the rivers of Ireland. He was most particular that we all include the sentence, "From the dizzy heights of the Boyne Bridge, the boats below looked like water beetles". I would love to have seen the marker's face as he went through all our English essays that year, as it was included in every single essay. He must have hidden behind one of the partitions, because when the adjudicator (or overseer if that is the correct title) left the room for a few minutes, Ryan appeared as if by magic asking if we needed help with spelling or anything else. I thought this was a bit inconsistent with his classroom habit of punishing boys who cheated, but I think that he was more concerned about how bad results would reflect on his teaching than he was about the boys. When he told me I had passed some days later I was pleased because it meant my schooldays were over though I was not yet thirteen years old. I would have liked to continue at school, but not at St Joseph's as Ryan's was the top class and I could not improve my education there. Ideally I am sure that at that time I needed to get away from there if I was to stand a chance of getting a secondary education.

Though my days no longer included lessons, there was no prospect of release from "Quentin" until my sixteenth birthday, unless my home circumstances were to change dramatically. Sadly, such likelihood was remote. I continued to sleep in the dormitory and remained at the mercy of the Brothers throughout the day, but my waking hours were now spent in other pursuits, of which more in due course. My father continued to make his monthly visits, and he always took us out to the town and bought a meal for us, but things had not changed at home and we were reluctant to pressure him to take us away from there.

Meanness with No Purpose

One Saturday, Dad arrived as usual to collect us, and we were getting ready to leave when one of the boys said Brother Acton wanted to see us both in the kitchen. We knew Acton was a Tuam man, and though we never had any dealings with him we always assumed that he would be friendly towards people from Tuam. I said "Sir, Dad has arrived to take us out to the town", and I could hardly believe my ears when he said, "You two are going nowhere today". We had never exchanged a single word with him since the day we arrived at the school, as he always worked in the kitchen and rarely left it. He said, "Tell your father he will have to call some other time, as I need you both today to peel potatoes". I had never done any work in the kitchen, and in fact I had never been inside its door since the day I arrived at the school. I saw Dad coming up the path and he said, "I have come for my boys". Acton, who stood about five foot four, answered, "Well, you cannot have them". My father, who was a giant of a man, laughed and said "They are my sons, and I am going to take them out to the town". Acton, with a look of pure venom, said, "I am going to call the police. You surrendered all rights the day you sent them here." I thought for a moment that Dad would hit the awful little man, but Dad for all his giant stature would never hit a smaller man than himself, especially one in a monk's habit. We managed to cool Dad down and told him we were not bothered about missing our monthly meal, knowing the poor man could not beat the system, yet only someone living on the muck they called food in St Joseph's would know how we had looked forward to our meal. I have dwelt long and often on the happenings of that day and I always arrive at the same conclusion. I feel sure that Acton was asked by one of the Brothers to carry out this spiteful act because after Dad's departure we were told to return to the playground. From that day to the day I departed that educational emporium I never peeled a potato. Nor indeed was I ever asked to do so.

The internal politics of the place were very complex and difficult to understand, and some of the Brothers openly detested each other. The boys too spoke in a lingo of their own, a language that I have never heard before or since, Heaven only knows how or when it was started or by whom.

To the present day I do not know how they managed to put so many sub humans in charge of over two hundred boys under one roof. It would appear now on looking back that a special type of Christian Brother was selected to staff the Industrial schools, with a mean streak a priority, They were nothing like the fine body of men who taught us in St Patrick's in Tuam. I can say with complete honesty that in the four years that I spent there I never came across one boy that I could call bad or evil. Perhaps the Clergy at that time saw evil everywhere they looked. I was told that a Brother Mullen from the Tuam school had been transferred to St Joseph's in Galway, and I would have loved to know how he responded, or if there was something in the Galway air that turned people into sadists. He was highly regarded by the boys in Tuam C. B. S.10 and I cannot understand how such a nice man ended up in "San Quentin". Perhaps he overstepped the mark and upset someone in authority.

Learning a Trade

I was now in 'no mans land', and was given a little time to decide which trade I wished to follow. It was the custom to put boys in my position to work in the short term doing odd jobs. I was told to push a handcart to the Great Southern Hotel and collect large drums of beef dripping and to return with it to the school promptly. It was then melted down, and a plateful issued to each boy to dip his dry bread in at breakfast. This was the only breakfast I ever was given during my time at St Joseph's, except on Easter Sunday when we were given our annual egg, boiled rock hard with hundreds of others in the big boiler. This was done under the watchful eye of Brother Gaynor, a big Kerry man whose favourite trick was to clip one on the ear if you came within range of his long reach. I got many a clip on the ear from him as did many other boys, and always for no reason. In fairness, however, I must say that Gaynor was not too bad and it was said often that he was not all there, and the other Monks made fun of him behind his back.

I was elevated to the position of Prefect around this time, a position that carried few privileges, except that one could on occasion steal a loaf of bread from the store to which I now had access. The trick was to stick a knife through it and pin it to the boards under the table, which I often managed for a few friends and myself. Not surprisingly my circle of friends increased considerably following my promotion.

I was called before Brother Ryan one day, and he informed me that a position was available in the cart-maker's workshop and wanted to know if I was interested. I was very keen to become a carpenter, as there was no prospect of furthering my education at the school so I said yes. The cart-maker was a Mr O' Connor, and it was obvious even to my inexperienced eye that he was a wonderful tradesman and a gentleman who was as pleasant with the young lads as he was with the Brothers. I spent many happy hours in his workshop, and it helped to distract me from my unpleasant surroundings, where nothing had changed since my first day in captivity.

I continued to progress under the watchful eye of the boxing instructor Sgt Brennan, and I was no longer picked on by the bullies I encountered when I first arrived. We were taken to Silver Strand to swim twice weekly every summer by O'Malley, who took great pride in his swimming ability. He was also a fitness fanatic, and he was contemptuous of any boy who was less than one hundred percent fit. I have often wondered if he was expecting me, 'T.B.' Joyce, to die from the dreaded disease he was convinced I suffered from. If so he must have been disappointed. I don't feel any gratitude to O'Malley as apart from the regular beatings I suffered at his hands, I was nearly always selected to go for a swim by him on Christmas morning, hardly the best treatment for a boy with T.B. Galway Bay is a chilly place to swim in summertime, never mind on a bitter cold Christmas morning.

I have often wondered how one teacher could have single-handedly acted as swimming instructor, lifeguard and supervisor to over sixty boys, most of whom could not swim. I can recall a few close calls, one of which concerned my brother John. We were told to take our swimming trunks, (if you could call the rough garments knocked together by the boys in the tailor's shop "trunks"), with us on our forced Sunday walk. When we got as far as Barna, (roughly seven miles away), we were told to get into our swimming gear and swim. O'Malley, who was a powerful swimmer, then swam far out to sea and during that period there was no supervision. It was due more to luck than anything that no one was drowned as he swam out of sight. When he arrived back, he shouted to the boys to get dressed, and then ordered us to line up in fours for the march back to the school. It was only then that someone shouted "Sir, there are three boys missing", and we were instructed to spread out to look for them. We heard shouting in the distance and saw the missing three cut off by the incoming tide. It took a few of the senior boys linking hands with O'Malley to rescue them from what would have been certain death. I will never understand how a fatality never occurred and I can only say that someone must have been watching over us all. I often heard my brother talk of the terror of that day, and it made me more careful not to go into deep water after that.

I worked in Mr O Connor's workshop with a few other lads, some of whom had no aptitude for the work and some no interest, but we all played tricks on "Tommo", as we called him. One day, the boys put some dog dirt with a drawing pin embedded in it on the door latch, and Tommo on attempting to press the latch down jabbed his thumb and instinctively stuck it into his mouth. His response was to make us do extra work causing us to miss football practice, but Tommo never remained angry for long and the boys probably liked him better than any other member of staff. I can see him now in my mind's eye giving the final touches to a new horse cart, and if a better craftsman ever lived than old "Tommo" I would like to meet him. I doubt if a cartmaker could be found today were you to search the length and breadth of Ireland.

I was now into my third year in St Joseph's and doing well in the cart makers shop, and though I quite enjoyed the work I longed for the day when the carpenter's shop would re open and I could get a transfer. I was kept busy however alternating between my weekly trips on the gravy train as I called my visits to the Hotel to collect the dripping, and the new job of taking the wheels to the blacksmith to be shod.

The blacksmith was called Mr Tom Flanagan and he was a master of his trade, which was to fit the iron rims on the new cartwheels, and the smaller hoops on the centre stock. This was a big job and it could not be rushed, so when I pushed the handcart to Tom Flanagan's, it meant that I was there for the day. He heated the steel rims and then he sweated them on to the wheels as he called the exercise, and I never tired of watching this skilled craftsman at work. He was typical of the picture people paint in their minds of the traditional blacksmith, with broad shoulders and powerful arms. I was always well fed by this good man who always spoke badly of the Brothers, and called them savages. I have no doubt he had heard all about the goings on at the school from many different boys over the years, and his assistant, another giant of a man, said those tyrants should be in jail. It seemed to be the opinion of anyone who was kind to the inmates of that awful place, and once or twice while pushing the handcart; people stopped and gave me a little money. If my dad had seen how low his son had sunk, it would have broken his heart.

One day as I was on my way to the cart maker's shop having just finished dinner, Brother Ryan called me over, and I wondered what it was about this time. When you were called to his presence, you jumped to obey and did not ask questions. I was told not to return to the shop that afternoon as he had other work in mind for me, and he bade me follow him to the recreation hall. When I got there the boy who was known as the barber, as it was his job to trim the hair of upwards of two hundred boys every month, was busy at his work. He had been doing the haircutting since I arrived at St Joseph's, and woe betide any boy who upset him as he had been known to take revenge with his clippers and scissors. Ryan said, "He will be going out next week". This in the school slang meant he would be leaving, and he said, "I want you to take over his duties". I said "I don't want to be a barber, Sir, and I am doing well in the cart makers shop", and he replied "You will do as I say, and you can easily combine the two jobs". He told me to start right away as I had only a week to learn the job and he instructed the regular barber to give me a crash course of training. I found out that afternoon that I quite enjoyed the work, and to my surprise I soon became quite expert at it in a short time.

I found it a break from doing the same job every day and it only took up three days in every month, he assured me. I cannot recall the other barber's name but he pointed out that I was now in a position of power, and that there were many advantages to be gained. Some of the older lads were very particular about how they wanted their hair cut, and made sure to keep in his good books, and I drew up a short list in my mind of the people who had given me a hard time when I first arrived at the school. I had a few accounts to settle and I levelled a few scores in the first few days, as it was I thought the best possible time, as someone who was new to the job would be expected to make a few mistakes. One fellow in particular who went out of his way to make life difficult for me was an early victim. I did a neat job on the front of his hair, but the back was like a meadow when the after grass starts to grow. I was delighted when he returned with tears in his eyes and begged me to correct it, but I pointed out that I was only learning the job and perhaps I would be able to do a better job next time, and there was great hilarity among the boys who had suffered at his hands. The next week he asked if I would like to borrow the "Champion" comic when he had read it. It was the most popular lad's comic at that time - I wonder if it is still printed. It was amazing how popular one became when you wielded a little power, but I can honestly say that I never took advantage after I had enacted my revenge. I continued to cut the boys' hair until I left, and I am certain that I could have made a living as a barber if I so desired.

It never occurred to me that I was due to leave when Brother Fahy instructed me to train another lad, and I did in fact go out into the world two weeks afterwards.

In the late summer a new man arrived to run the carpenter's shop and I was transferred to work with him. He was called Mr Kennedy, and I liked him from the start. He was a good tradesman, and he taught me a lot about my trade. The long nights were drawing in, and being poorly clothed we felt the bitter cold in the evenings as we were made to stay out in the yard. The Brothers, of course, stayed in the warmth of the big hall, as my brother and I sat close together on the seats that were attached to the outer wall to try and keep warm. I am afraid we both ended in tears one evening as we talked of our home and our dead sister, and how she was taken from us at thirteen years of age. Two sad little boys recounted the happy times when our mother was alive, and we tried to console each other by planning what we would do when we were released.

CHAPTER 6

A Winter to Remember

It was not unusual to hear children crying on those cold evenings as they struggled to get warm in the freezing schoolyard, and as a mature adult I often feel my eyes fill up still when my mind wanders back. If I live to be a hundred, I do not expect to endure another winter as cold as that one. Certainly in what is now my seventy-first year, I cannot recall a winter as severe as nineteen forty-seven. I can still recall the agony of the burst chilblains on the backs of my fingers, which I dared not scratch, no doubt caused by lack of nourishment and malnutrition while the Brothers remained indifferent to the suffering. I can truthfully say that O'Malley continued to regularly dish out his six of the best to anyone who annoyed him, and on frozen hands too. I am convinced that he got some sort of turn-on from inflicting pain on the helpless and the weak.

When bedtime came we were ushered into the bitter cold dormitories, which were unheated. There were radiators in every dormitory but they were barely more than lukewarm, and I am convinced that the bulk of the heat was directed to the monks' quarters. There was a form of entertainment of course- there was an opening in the dividing wall between the two large dormitories where a radio was situated, and I can readily recall a popular

59

programme called "Around the fire". This was broadcast twice a week and featured a wonderful accordion player called Albert Healey, and on occasion we were allowed to listen to a play. Lights out was at ten o clock when John Judge took up his night watchman duties, and I can recall some boys being beaten ten or fifteen minutes later for being awake. I have yet to meet a person- child or adult- that can fall asleep to order.

The football season always started on St Patrick's Day, weather permitting, and was a welcome break from a winter in the schoolyard. The Railway Cup football and hurling finals were always played on that day, and the whole country tuned in to hear the golden voice of Michael O' Hehir as he relayed the happenings in Croke Park to any home lucky enough to own a radio. I remember the Connacht hurling team represented by fifteen Galway men, beating a strong Leinster side to reach the final against Munster who were regarded as being unbeatable at that time .It was a great disappointment to everyone when the final was delayed until Easter Sunday because of bad weather. Brother Ryan promised to lay on a party if Connacht won, knowing there was little or no chance of this happening. I can see the boys' faces when the impossible happened and Galway won, beating Munster, captained by Christy Ring with the Mackey brothers in their forward line.

Nearly sixty years have gone by since that magical day when fifteen Galway men proved themselves better than the cream of Munster, and will I ever forget the names of my boyhood heroes? How could any inmate of St Joseph's never forget the great Sean Duggan, the prince of goalkeepers, Josie Gallagher, James Killeen and peerless Paddy Gantley? I could name them all, but anyone who participated in the gleeful cheers and shouts of "Party, party", will remember the sickly grin on Ryan's big red face as he was made to keep his promise. I must confess that the party itself was forgettable as it consisted of a glass of lemonade and a piece of currant cake for each of us, but it tasted better than any I have eaten since because we had put one over on Ryan. It would be hard to forget that glorious day when the habitual losers won and Munster lost.

We were, like most youngsters in our age group, taking an interest in all sports, especially rugby. I think this was because at that time Ireland was doing well on the international rugby field. It was a relatively new game for the majority of our people at that time, as indeed was golf. They were games that were played mostly by the ruling classes or the people that came of plantation stock known to the native Irish as 'The Ascendancy', or 'The Quality' as they were called by the poorer classes. The Christian Brothers preached that we should never stoop to play the games of the invader, though they themselves on occasion had been known to play a round of golf .The game of tennis was never mentioned.

One day a boy called Flaherty shouted, "I heard Jacky Kyle has scored for Ireland", and was immediately given a severe thrashing by Brother Ryan. Kyle was our one and only super star and was rated by experts as the best outside half in the world. It was not surprising that boys should take an interest in how their national team was faring, but we were not allowed to show an interest or even talk about the game. I am afraid that telling boys that it was against the national interest to play or even talk about the game of rugby was taking things too far, especially as Ireland was as at that stage just beginning to hold its own at international level. I was sent to the big dormitory to collect a book for one of the teachers some time later, and you can imagine my surprise when I found three of the Brothers listening to the rugby broadcast on the dormitory radio. Talk of hypocrites!

From Bad to Bad

It was often said amongst the boys that Ryan had a lady friend who used to visit him in his room, so when he disappeared one day never to be seen again at St Joseph's, word went around that he had been thrown out of the Order. Some said he had married the lady, but we were never to find out. His replacement arrived as I entered my last year in the school, and the first thing he did was to close down the boxing club. Needless to say we were all bitterly disappointed. The sad thing was that Sgt Brennan had just reached the pinnacle of success as a trainer with one of the boys from the school being crowned all Ireland champion. Brother Fahy was no improvement on Ryan and if anything was more severe in enforcing a more rigid discipline. I had grown to love boxing and I was determined to return to the Ring as soon as I left the school, and I planned to join the Tuam boxing Club when I returned home.

Fahy announced his arrival at St Joseph's by calling an assembly and telling us that he would find a manlier pastime for us than boxing. Perhaps he knew something that the rest of us did not know, but I have yet to find such a pastime. He strutted the yard like a sergeant major shouting at all and sundry. His favourite name for anyone who annoyed him was youls which translated from the Irish I think means devils. I thought this a bit much from a man who spent most of his time shouting out abuse at the boys, and described boxing as a sport for thugs and roughnecks. He was a big fat red faced bully who could be very violent, and in the company of a handful of boys who climbed a wall to help ourselves to a few apples, I was severely punished. The apples grew in a field to the rear of a builder's yard beside the football field, and were always left to rot, so we climbed the low wall and took an apple each. We were very hungry, having eaten a less than satisfactory dinner when Fahy spotted us, and having first told us we would go straight to hell he then knocked hell out of us. I knew a few lads who would have gladly swapped a little while there to escape from that tyrant.

I remember on one occasion when Fahy, who fancied himself as a very good detective, discovered a new shoe was missing from the stores, and as it was a left shoe he got the bright idea that a one legged boy whose right leg was missing, was the guilty one and to his delight he was right. That day that poor lad more than paid for his crime. If only he had taken the pair.

Shortly after the arrival of Brother Fahy, or 'the quare fellow' as the boys called him, a lad who had left the school about a year or so before Fahy's arrival returned to St Joseph's. This poor lad had gone to work for someone and he had apparently lost his job and he was in a very distressed state .He was in desperate need of help, as he had no money to buy food and he was very poorly clothed. I heard it said by one boy who had been his friend before he left the school, that he had been ill treated by a drunken employer who owed him a few weeks' wages. He seemed a very sad soul when Fahy called him out to stand in front of the boys at assembly. It was evident to us from the start that Fahy set out to humiliate the poor youth, who must have really been at his wits' end to return to that horrible school. "I want everyone present to take a good look at what I call one of life's losers", he said. "We prepared him as indeed we prepare all of you to go out in the world and bring credit on your school, and what you see before you is our reward for years of hard work". The poor lad broke down in tears as Fahy screamed "Get out of my sight". I did not see him again, but I saw a few other unfortunates unlucky enough to have to return to "San Quentin", and they in their turn felt the weight of the quare fellow's tongue.

When I eventually got to mix with normal people in later years, I began to realise that we the inmates of the

64

Industrial school had become brainwashed into accepting brutality and beatings as the norm. I found it very strange, especially when I first worked in England, to find the English so much nicer to work for than our own people. I mean it was both a pleasure and a surprise to find a race that had inflicted so much pain on our people over the centuries, went out of their way to help you enjoy your day's work. I find it very easy to get on with English people and indeed my wife is English born. I ask myself over and over why we have had so much conflict between the two races and I always arrive at the same conclusion: there is good and bad in every race, and if the Irish were judged by the Christian Brothers in St Joseph's school, our name would stink throughout the world.

Dad's Surprise

My dad continued to visit every four weeks, but I nearly collapsed in shock when he greeted us with the words, "Well boys I got married since I last saw you both". We stared at him dumfounded and we could not speak for a few seconds, then he said "She is a relation of an old friend and lived with her bachelor brother and they don't get on. It is a marriage of convenience for both of us. She is a very kind person and we will bring you both home shortly". My brother and myself were stuck for words. When I met her brother at a later date I thought it very strange that my stepmother could not get along with him. If a nicer man existed I had yet to meet him, and yet my stepmother went out of her way to help my brother and myself. Her true character would be revealed to us before we were much older, to the utter dismay of my poor father.

I was still in the care of the good Christian Brothers however, and had yet to meet up with the lady who could not get along with her brother. I must confess that when I did eventually meet up with her and got to know her, my thoughts were "out of the frying pan into the fire."

St Joseph's was preparing for confirmation day, when the bishop would visit the school to confirm those who were not yet confirmed. It was a special occasion that only occurred every few years, so a special effort was being made, with every boy given a job to do. A local builder was employed to erect new bases to carry flowerpots in the area in front of the classrooms, and a painter and decorator was given the task of painting the outer walls of the buildings a bright colour. I got to talk with this man one day and discovered to my delight that he was none other than the great Tom Fleming, a man I had often read about but never expected to meet. Tom had starred on the Galway hurling team that had captured our only All Ireland title back in nineteen twenty-three but was now almost ready to retire. I felt privileged to have met this hero of my youth.

The work neared completion as the big day drew near, and woe betide any boy who dropped litter or paper in the school yard. Brother Fahy told us about how important confirmation was, and pointed out that everyone took another name when they were confirmed, in addition to the names they were given when christened. He then went on to say you will all take Joseph in honour of our school's patron saint. I had been confirmed in Tuam, but my brother, who was too young at the time, had been christened John Joseph shortly after being born, and he pointed this out to Fahy. The red faced tyrant shouted, "You will take Joseph", and so it came to pass that my brother is called John Joseph Joseph. I often wonder how many boys are so named as I think most of the Industrial Schools are called St Joseph's. This was an act of lunacy even by the standards of that hellhole, and I decided that day that hell was on earth and staffed by devils in Monks' habits. I often wonder how Fahy never had a stroke, as he was always angry at someone, and his blood pressure must have passed safe limits.

We were finally allowed home for two weeks in early summer, a privilege I suppose denied boys who had committed some offence or other. We of course had done no wrong, and I must say that it was something unheard of in my time there for boys to be allowed home on holiday. I then met my stepmother for the first time, and she seemed delighted to see us, and gave us a little money to spend. It was very strange being allowed to sleep late in the mornings, and not hearing Langan's abusive shouts of "Get up get up and get washed". We had just got used to the home comforts when it was time to return to Galway, but we knew dad was arranging for our release so it was not too painful. I had found it difficult to mix with some of my old pals who seemed to give me a wide berth as if I had some form of leprosy. I was very confused, as I could not decide whether it was because they thought I had T.B. or because I was in an Industrial School.

I was somewhat relieved to return to the school, and I had thought the rooms at home much smaller than I remembered, probably because of the enormous rooms at the school .Dad had bought some new clothes for us during our time at home and remarked on how poorly we were dressed, and he got very angry when we told him how Ryan had taken our new clothes from us when we arrived in Galway. It crossed my mind that perhaps my friends had avoided me because I was so poorly dressed .I will never know the truth, but in fairness to those boys they soon accepted me as one of their own when I finally returned to live in Tuam. I had overlooked the fact that at that time I was almost a stranger to them, having been away from home for a few years, but the young are very sensitive and easily hurt.

Another Surprise

One morning as I was coming out from mass I saw the quare fellow Fahy coming towards me, and my first thought was 'which rule have I broken now'. To my amazement something I had not seen before happened, and his big red face broke into a smile. "And how we are this fine morning, young man". I was so shocked it took me a moment to answer and I replied "Well sir thank you". He then said "Step into the kitchen, I want to talk to you", and to my amazement he ordered two cups of tea. He then went on to describe a great job he had in mind for me, and said it was "only a few miles from your home town". He told me that I would be working for a carpenter, a friend of the carpenter who worked at the school, Mr Kennedy, who had recommended me, and I would be paid twelve shillings a week and my keep. "I have had favourable reports from Mr Kennedy about your progress in the carpenters shop", he said, "and I think it is time to give some thought to your future". He continued in this manner, and if I did not know better I would have been convinced that concern for my future welfare was uppermost in his mind .He said that Mr Kennedy was putting a lot of faith in me and he was confident that I would not let him down, and he went on to remind me that the good name of the school must be upheld at all costs. He said that we were standard bearers from the day we left St Joseph's, and that I should always remember what the school had done for me. I solemnly assured him that I was never likely to forget what it had done for me, nor am I likely to as the marks are still there. This brute, who had made a career out of punishing young defenceless children, was concerned lest the outside world find out about the brutality that went on there. There was little or no chance of this happening because at that time to speak ill of the good Monks was akin to sacrilege. I was so relieved to be getting away that I thought I had better not overdo the sarcasm, though it went straight over his head.

I had been in trouble a short time before this for complaining when each boy was given half a crown to go to the annual Galway race meeting, as it cost that amount to get to the Square, and as much again to get to the racecourse. There was a little matter of finding something to eat, and young people get hungry often, and when a few returned to the school requesting food they were refused. They knocked at the kitchen door starving only to be told to clear off and not to return until after six o'clock. I believe the smell of roast lamb was overpowering. I was told on that occasion that as head boy I should be on the side of authority so at that moment I did not wish to upset his highness.

Twelve shillings a week may seem a laughable sum today, but in nineteen forty-eight to a boy who never had any money it seemed a lot. I was only given a few minutes to say farewell to my brother, but I was not allowed to say goodbye to my friends. I was given ten shillings and put on a bus to a village a few miles from Tuam, where the man who was to become my first employer met me. This man turned out to be a swine to his toenails if I ever met one. I was treated like his dog except that his dog was not required to work ten hours a day and was shown a lot of kindness. I cannot say the same about his family however, and to my dying day I will remember the kindness shown to me by his father, mother and sister. I was to meet his brother later that week, a blacksmith by trade and a fine decent man, who could not have treated me any better had I been a family member.

On meeting my new employer, I was shaken warmly by the hand, and he then introduced me to the rest of the family. I was very impressed by the friendliness of their greeting. He was a young unmarried man in his middle twenties, and he said he would take me to see the workshop after dinner. I am afraid I was not very impressed by the stable he called a workshop, as it was the end stable in a line of three. It only measured roughly fifteen feet by ten, and was a far cry from the workshop at the school. He then went on to explain that he had not much work at the moment but this was unusual, and would I mind doing a couple of days on the farm, to which I readily agreed. I was just happy to be away from the good Christian Brothers, and I looked forward to having a little money of my own at weekend. I was put to work, haymaking, spreading turf, mucking out the cow byres and countless other jobs on the farm.

I was a little disappointed as a couple of days turned to a full working week, and I looked forward to working at my trade the next week. I must confess I wondered how he could carry out a carpentry business in such a small place, and I noticed that the floor sloped outwards about eight inches. We went to mass on Sunday and afterwards he asked if I played football and I told him I did. He then said to a man who was talking to a few other men, "I have got a new midfield man and he is willing to play for us". I was only too willing to try myself out against the visiting team and though I think we lost they said I had played well. I thought the standard of play not very good, and one did not need to be a star player to look fairly good. Mr O`Donnell would have had a heart attack had he seen the lack of teamwork and skill, but there was no shortage of energy and a few were injured but not seriously. I was pleased that I was able to stand up to much older boys and more than able to hold my own.

I thought my employer had forgotten to pay me but I was shy about mentioning it, and I was nearly reduced to tears when he said "You may have helped a bit on the farm but you have done nothing for me". I had arranged to go to the local dance hall that evening with a few of the football team, and I would have to forget about it as I expected to get paid and I was depending on my first week's wages. The family asked if I was going to the dance and I made some excuse or said I was tired, I cannot remember which after all those years. Monday came and still no mention of work and the old man asked me if I had been paid, and when I said no he muttered "the bastard".

I helped at haymaking and at saving turf for a few more days, and his father, a lovely old man, gave me some money. I was talking to a few local lads one evening at the gate of the house, and as I looked around suddenly my employer (if I can call him that), was making fun of me behind my back. I saw red and asked him what was so funny, and he replied "You are the only person in the village with a criminal record". Though I was not yet sixteen I was a big lad and I had developed into a very good boxer, and I could not take much more from him. I moved away from him into the open space where his strength and weight were of no advantage and said "Come on you bastard, let your friends see what you are made of". On reflection I think that Mr Kennedy may have told him that I was a boxer, because he first shaped up as if ready for battle then seemed to have a rapid change of mind. He said "Ah forget it Steve, sure I was only joking". I did not think much of his sense of humour but I was glad that no blows were struck, because I would surely have hammered him, and I thought it would look good, the Industrial Schoolboy being sent back to Galway in disgrace. I can only imagine the treatment I would have received from the holy Monks if it were reported that I had beaten up my boss, and I am sure they would only have heard his side of the story. I think they would have forgotten to mention that he was a grown man and I a lad of fifteen years and a few months. I am afraid the Ireland of the nineteen forties gave no rights to an Industrial School inmate, regardless of why you were there, or whether you were right or wrong.

CHAPTER 7

Return to Tuam

It suddenly dawned on me that I was no better off than I had been in 'San Quentin', and I thought the sooner I got away from the place the better. I lost no time making up my mind what to do, as there was no point in delaying my departure now that I had decided to leave. I always got up early from years of habit, so no one noticed anything strange, and I packed my few belongings before setting out on foot for Mountbellew town. I had to travel on foot because I had barely enough money for my bus fare to Tuam. I would have had more than enough money had I been paid what I was due .My father was surprised to hear that I had left my good job. Brother Fahy had assured him of how lucky I was to have got it when he went to collect my brother, who had started in the local Technical school in Tuam on his return from Galway.

John finished his schooling unlike myself, and has remained in Tuam where he later married. He still resides there and his family has made a success of their lives. I explained to Dad my reason for leaving my job, and I had to beg him not to go there and 'break my ex-boss's head', as he put it. Though he was a big powerful man he was slow to anger, but when he heard how I was treated he looked mad enough to kill someone. I was just happy to be home again and delighted to have a dad who was prepared to stick up for his son.

It was great also to renew old friendships after over four years away from home, and to my delight I got a job right away working for a local carpenter. This man who was a friend of my father was employed by a contracting company in town, and was a first class tradesman who ran a business making hospital bedside lockers. He offered me a job right away at double what I should have been paid in my first job, (though of course I never did get paid). I got on great with this man who was delighted with my work, and I was only required to work eight hours a day instead of ten. I had already outgrown the clothes I had been given leaving Galway, and I was now able to buy some new things with my own money. I started going to the local dances, joined the football and boxing clubs and my life had suddenly improved more than I ever expected.

When my job making the lockers finished, my boss got a job for me with his employer, who at that time was probably the biggest contractor in town. It was common knowledge in the town that this man was unskilled and what today would be called a chancer, but to hear him boast he was the best carpenter in Ireland. He had all the qualifications to become a member of staff at St Joseph's; in short, he was a swine. He reminded me so much of Paddy Langan by the brutal treatment he dished out to people who could not afford to lose their jobs by answering him back. It was hard to believe that this man, who was highly thought of in the town as a daily mass goer and communicant, was the same tyrant who bullied and swore at his unfortunate workmen six days a week. When he retired I am sure his slaves were overjoyed that he could spend more time in church taking care of his immortal soul.

I was now settling down to going to work daily, and in spite of my intense dislike of my employer, a dislike shared by all who worked for him, I was for the first time since my mother's death living a near normal life. I can only imagine how a convict must feel when he is released after having served a long term in prison, and I think I can relate a little to how he must feel by saying it was good to be alive and free. I was probably able to endure my employer's tyranny better than my fellow workers because I had four years training in St Joseph's, and I was beginning to believe that all employers were swine. The only change I noticed was that I got paid every Friday, and I always looked forward to weekends and football practice, and of course the Sunday night dance. At first I found it difficult to mix with young people of my own age, until a girl asked me to dance in a 'ladies' choice', and I managed to get through it without walking all over her feet. I had broken the ice, and from there on I started to make friends.

True Colours

One Sunday morning as we congregated around the old cross in the square after mass, discussing the counties' football fortunes, someone mentioned that the trials for the County minor team were to be held that afternoon in Park More. One lad said he had received a letter inviting him to go for a trial, and a couple of others said that they also had got invitations. I thought I might take my football strip and chance getting a game. I knew that I had no chance of ever playing for the County, and I had only ever played one competitive game other than at the school, and that was for a village team.

I went to the football pitch that afternoon and saw the great Tull Dunne, (the star of Galway when they had won 'All Irelands' in better times long gone) conducting the trials .He called out the names of the 'probables', and all answered "Here". He then called out the names of the 'possibles', and when he came to right half forward, there was no reply. The great man looked around and asked "Is there a wing forward present?" and I put my hand up. He asked my name, and handed me the number ten jersey.

My knees were knocking as the teams took the field, but I soon settled down and played quite well, though I had never played in that position before. I bought the Tuam Herald on Tuesday evening and looked to see if any of the Tuam lads had made the county team. I thought I was seeing things when I saw S. Joyce had been picked at right half forward for the County - there was a God in heaven after all. I ran home to break my good news to my family, and the greeting I got from my stepmother was shocking and most unexpected.

She started screaming as soon as I walked in the door, "What do you mean walking in here twenty minutes late for your dinner, do you think I am your slave?" I did not eat any dinner that evening. My stepmother had shown her true colours, and I fully understood when I got to know the good man, why her brother Thady referred to her as 'that screaming banshee'. It spoiled what was a wonderful occasion for me having been selected to wear the famous maroon and white of Galway and finding Dad had married a bitch. I got up for work the next morning to be greeted by my smiling stepmother, and she acted as though yesterday's events had never happened. I finished my breakfast and I set out for work with a heavy heart. The world I was beginning to enjoy was not the nice place I had thought it was. I was introduced to her brother Thady a few days later and we hit it off from the minute we met. He was a wonderful character in an old fashioned way. I have made many friends over the years that I regard very highly, and this man is up there with the best. I feel no shame in admitting that I cried when he died. On the other hand we never knew which stepmother would greet us in the mornings.

Good Clean Fun!

I looked forward to my first game for Galway nervously. It was a big step up in class from playing in the city schools' league, and the thought of wearing the same colours as the great Sean Purcell, Frankie Stockwell and Jackie Mangan was like a dream. We were due to play Sligo in the first round of the Connacht minor championship, or the under eighteens as we were sometimes known. The day arrived and I waited nervously to meet my new team mates and they soon put in an appearance, among them the great St Jarlaths college star Jack Mahon, who would star on the Galway team who became All Ireland champions in nineteen fifty six. St Jarlath's college has long been the leading nursery for Gaelic football in the Country, and I suppose it was understandable that the Industrial School boy felt overawed. To the present day I do not know if Jack Mahon or any of the others knew my background, but I can truthfully say that they all treated me as an equal on that day long ago, and I still count Jack and the rest among my friends today.

The long awaited moment arrived, and I trotted out on to St Coleman's Park with the rest of the Galway team. It would be nice to report that we won, but Sligo beat us by a narrow margin. I was told that I had played well before suffering an injury to my ankle half way through the second half. There was no need to be downhearted as I had achieved more before my sixteenth birthday than most footballers do in their careers. My father and brother were proud that a Joyce had played for the County if only at the lowest level, but to hear Thady my step uncle boasting of my prowess you would think I was up there with Purcell, Mangan, and Stockwell.

I often laugh when I hear people talk about football hooligans today. Today's hooligans are only amateurs compared to some of the characters I saw in action at junior Gaelic football games when I was a lad. On one occasion a friend of mine who is now sadly no longer with us was asked to referee a match between two parish teams, and the inevitable fight broke out just on half time. Dan (for that was his name) went home for his tea and left the combatants to get on with the fight. He returned after a long rest, blew his whistle to clear the field and got on with the game. No one thought anything was amiss.

One gentleman who was neutral liked to go around the outer fringes of the fight, pick the biggest guy he could see, hang a haymaker on his chin and run like hell. Good clean fun was had by all and not a hooligan to be seen. Happy days.

I recall another happening in Tuam many years ago when I think it was the Galway three in a row team (they won three All Irelands in a row) were playing Dublin in a National League play off, and the winner's prize was to be a trip to America. One Galway man who shall be nameless got involved in a bout of fisticuffs with a Dublin gentleman who took exception to too loud applause for Galway's fourth goal. As the 'Dub', unkindly called a Jackeen by the wearer of a maroon and white badge, swung a haymaker, the Culthie (unkind name for anyone born outside Dublin) ducked neatly and floored the Jackeen with a left hook. The Jackeen swung his left foot to a delicate part of the Galwayman's anatomy from his prone position, only to have the trouser leg removed from his Sunday best and thrown into the crowd. The Galway supporters expertly fielded it as it sped on its way never to be seen again by its anguished owner. The Tuam sergeant for some unknown reason locked our hero up for the night, and released him without charge the next morning. I think he was punished for passing some uncomplimentary remarks about Culthies, when he was accused of stealing a suit from a one legged man. Last seen he was thumbing a lift on the Dublin road with the morning's paper wrapped around his bare hoof. One eye was noticeably darker than the other.

I was keeping my eyes open hoping I might get lucky and get a better job, but at that time any kind of job was almost impossible to find in Tuam, or as the locals would say jobs were 'as rare as hen's teeth'. I was approached one day by a local carpenter, a man who owned the longest established company in town and his firm was renowned for the high quality of their work. He wanted to know if I would be interested in coming to work for him at a wage in excess of three times my present wage. I did not have to give it any thought and I accepted his offer on the spot, and I started work at my new job the following Monday. I tried to spend as little time as possible in our home as my stepmother's behaviour got more and more unstable, and now that I was earning good money I had started contributing a generous sum towards the housekeeping. Things came to a head one Friday evening when as I handed her my money, without warning she threw it into the fire. I tried to rescue my hard-earned wages but failed, and I decided on the spot that I would never give her another chance to repeat it.

I was now playing regularly for the town team, and we managed to get to the county semi-final where we met Jack Mahon and his team who defeated us in a hard fought game. I thought we could win it the following year as we had a young team, and we were a happy bunch of lads when in fact we did lift the cup after a hard final against a team from Galway city.

I had settled in well in my new job and I worked alongside the father of my employer - a man of over eighty years of age who did a full day's work, and was as good a worker as a man of half his age, and he taught me some of the skills for which he was renowned. He was probably the best craftsman I have ever met. He was capable of doing a good day's work, and he taught me a lot about my trade .He had been a lifelong member of the local coursing club and had always owned greyhounds, and even now at his advanced years he hoped to one day own a dog to win the Waterloo Cup .I am sorry to relate that he never realised his life's ambition.

I enjoyed some comical happenings whilst working with the old man. I recall on one occasion a giant of a man walked into the workshop leading a brindle greyhound, and enquired if the old boy was interested in buying the dog. He replied that he would not buy anything from the visitor who today would be called a traveller. I am afraid in those days he was called a tinker. "Who owns the dog?" he asked, and the tinker replied "He is mine. I was given the dog by a man who owed me a favour and I have his pedigree in my pocket which I can show you". He then produced the papers to prove he was not lying, and I could see the old fellow was interested. He finished up buying the greyhound for five pounds which was a lot of money in those days, and as they shook hands and he handed over the fiver he jokingly asked, "Would he kill a hare?" The tinker's reply was a classic. "He bloody would if he could catch him" he replied. Needless to say the dog was useless.

The old man took it well and said "some you win and some you lose", and when I got to know him better I found that he won a lot more than he lost. He told me many interesting stories, some about his youth, and one went like this. During the Anglo-Irish war two tinkers walked in to the workshop one day to enquire about a coffin, "Do you have a coffin large enough for a man of six foot four?" one asked. There was a rack by the wall with coffins of various sizes stacked on it, and the largest was six foot two. The two made a great show of deciding what they should do, and then went on to explain that Paddy had died and was in the camp down the Milltown road, and they were uncertain whether they could fit him in to a coffin only six foot two as he was a giant of six four. They then suggested that he allow them to take the coffin down to the camp and see if it was long enough. He told them he would work all night if a larger coffin was needed, and it would be ready by the next morning. They arrived back about ten minutes later and said it was too small, but they would go in to the town and see if they could buy a larger one- if not they would return and order one .He instructed them to put it back on the rack and they did as he requested and that was the last he saw of them. Two weeks later the dog was behaving strangely under the coffin racks, and there was a sickly smell in the area. They traced it and found it came from the six foot two coffin, and when they opened it the giant Paddy was in it -all five foot four of him. The old man assured me that it would be a waste of time trying to trace his nearest and dearest as they could be as far away as Dublin by now, and with the Black and Tans on the rampage and the I.R.A. blowing up bridges to frustrate the Tans, they had to decide what to do. They decided to hold a collection, and enough money was collected to give Paddy a good Christian burial and pay for a decent wake. The old boy swore this story was true and who am I to call him a liar.

Sometimes you cannot win

To get back to myself I was training hard for the forthcoming Connacht boxing championships, and I had a few fights and managed to win them all, so in confident

mood I set out for Castlebar. On my arrival I checked the
entries and saw that there were only two entries in the
heavyweight division, and several in the light heavy
entries, I thought quickly and decided it would be easier
to box as a heavyweight and I would only have to box
twice, or once if I got lucky in the draw. I was a small
light heavy, only twelve stone two pounds, and when I
told the clerk of the scales that I would box as a
heavyweight he said I was mad. I said, "We are all mad
to be knocking hell out of each other". I then pointed out
that there was no specified weight limit for heavyweight,
and he said, "it's your life that is at stake".

The draw was made a short while after that and to my
delight I saw that I had a bye straight in to the final. I sat
at ringside and watched two giants weighing each in
excess of fifteen stone knocking hell out of each other,
and I applauded every time one or other landed a
haymaker on his opponent. When the bout finished I
grinned as two exhausted heavyweights threw their arms
around each other's shoulders. I am no hero but I was
looking forward to the final. My opponent was one Billy
Healey who weighed fifteen stone four pounds and I am
sure my friends in the crowd said a few prayers for me.
The M. C. finished the introductions, the bell rang and I
was fighting for the heavyweight championship of
Connacht.

Healey came out like a tiger throwing murderous
punches, as I kept on the move. I had the advantage of
speed and a good left hand, which I kept in his face, and I

could not believe how easy it was. My confidence continued to grow as I gave him a boxing lesson and switched my attack to the body. I landed a terrific right to his body and the ref. said "Stop boxing, Joyce keep your punches up". I said, "that was not low", and I landed another body shot and I heard him grunt. The referee then issued a public warning to me. I was mad at the ref. because both punches were just under the heart, but I was not worried. I decided to keep working on the head and he could not call my punches low, but I should have known the referee would beat me when Healey could not. I landed a solid right to the head and opened a bad cut over his left eye, again the ref. told me to stop boxing and called the doctor. When the doctor stopped the contest as Healey was unable to continue, the ref. called a few officials over. The M. C. then announced that the Irish Amateur boxing association was experimenting with a new rule. He stated that if a man be stopped because of injury he should be awarded the verdict if he is ahead on points, and as I had the first round taken from me because of a public warning Healey was the winner. He was heavyweight champion and he had not landed a single punch. The crowd jeered and booed such blatant robbery, but I could do nothing about it - referees.

I will know until the day I die that I was the champion that night. I will always see the face of a young Englishman when he stopped his Irish opponent in the national stadium in Dublin only to be told that he had lost. I knew how that young man felt that evening when he won fair and square, stopping his opponent with a cut eye, only to be robbed by an official who probably never threw a punch in anger.

Thady

I was not very happy living under the same roof as my stepmother, so I started to spend as much time as possible down on the farm with Thady. I could not have felt any closer to the old boy if he had been a blood relation. My employer had allowed me to work on an extension to the local college to gain experience, which meant I had more free time to myself. The boxing club closed down for a short time during the summer months, but we were now into the Gaelic football season so we were kept busy training. I was selected to play for the Tuam senior team, and later on I made the county junior team and I felt on top of the world.

I enjoyed the work on the farm and every evening Thady kept myself and the young people of the neighbourhood entertained with tales of his youthful escapades. One tale went like this. Thady was on his way to a sheep fair in Dunmore in the early hours accompanied by a neighbour, and as they passed a tinker's camp, saw his bare backside protruding from under the canvas. Thady bet his companion a gallon of Guinness that he would not give the tinker's behind a belt with the ash plant he carried to control the sheep. His pal was something of an athlete, so he was prepared to give it a go. He removed his heavy boots, tied the laces together and hung them around his neck to ensure a quick get away. He spat on his fist, and taking careful aim he brought the ash plant down with an almighty crack on the sleeping tinker's behind. The tinker came alive with an unearthly roar, tearing the tent pegs from the ground as he took off after the flying Tom, known to all as 'The Flyer' for he was a good runner I believe. The fact that his wardrobe consisted of a shirt that only reached his navel never occurred to him as, with murderous intent, he closed on the flying Tom. He stood six foot four and Tom felt his Guinness-scented breath on his neck, and fear helped him to move up a gear. I believe the tinker ran out of gas probably because of an uncertain diet, and Tom was in Dunmore a long time before the bold Thady. Meanwhile the tinker returned to his residence to the amazement and amusement of early risers. Tom swore he would not do it again for all the Guinness in Dublin. I believe the gallon of Guinness cost Thady one shilling and four pence, less than fifteen pence in today's money. Those were the days. I am certain that it is a true story because Thady repeated it every time he was drunk, and that was often. Will we ever see your likes again Thady?

The local farmers loved his company and one of them once visited him as an old German watch maker was repairing an ancient wag of the wall clock that had been in the family for over a hundred years. He found the skeleton of a field mouse jammed in the mechanism; it had obviously found its way in from the thatch. He removed it and oiled the clock and it started up. It had no hour hand but that never bothered Thady who could tell the hour by just looking at the sun - he always got it right. Thady was in his usual spot at Lynch's bar after mass on Sunday when one of the locals, having heard about the clock repairer thought he would enjoy a laugh at Thady's expense. He asked "is it true that you brought a man over from Germany to repair the old clock?" "Quite true", answered Thady, "I did at great expense". "What was wrong with it?" asked the joker. "Ah Jasus" said Thady, "how the hell could it go, the engine driver was dead." (The old German had come to Ireland to get away from Hitler's Germany, and spent the war years going around the country repairing clocks and watches.)

One day Thady was approached by the local vet who was organising the agricultural show. Thady assumed there was a guaranteed that first prize in the offing, as the vet who was also a judge praised his new-born foal and said to make sure to enter it. He turned up on the day with the foal well groomed and its hooves polished. There were only four entries in the foal section and when third and second prizes were awarded Thady passed some extremely unkind remarks to the two owners about their animals, knowing he was going to get first prize. I feared the worst, and my fears were realised a few minutes later when the other foal was awarded the winner's rosette. The air turned blue, and some sedate ladies heard a few strange words they never saw in their prayer books. For a regular churchgoer he had a wide ranging vocabulary. He was to have the last word however, when he sold his foal at Ballinrobe horse fair a few days later, and it was announced as the first prize winner at Tuam show. It wore on it's bridle a rosette that had disappeared from the winners bridle in Tuam to the great annoyance of its owner. He got a good price for it too - he who laughs last. We were busy haymaking one day when an American stopped to enquire "where will this road take me". Thady replied "I have lived here seventy three years and it never took me anywhere". The American looked bemused, got into his car and slowly drove away. No one ever took offence as there was not one bit of malice in the old man, and his humour was that of a man who had lived through two world wars and the Black and Tan terror, yet still saw the funny side of life.

His grandfather was a tenant at will on the land, and he was not allowed to fatten a goose for Christmas by his absentee landlord. He once told me that a Major Veasey the landlord's agent or "a gombeen man" as the tenants called him would make unannounced visits, and if everything was not to his liking he could have you thrown off the land. We had been a subject race for over seven hundred years, and he had lived to see the changes his grandparents never thought could happen. There was a method of conveying a warning of the Major's impending visit so there was always time to remove the Christmas goose from sight. I wonder how the flyer Tom came to get his nickname.

CHAPTER 8

The Sporting Life

I was back working for my employer now that the college work was completed, and the knowledge I had acquired was to prove advantageous at a later date when I had departed my native shores. I was also boosting my income working as a bouncer at the local dance hall. It earned me a couple of extra pounds a week which was very handy, It was easy money as most of the lads knew me and gave no trouble, Now and again some fellow would get ambitious and I would try to talk some sense into him and only as a last resort would I throw him out. If any of the locals were short of funds I would let them in free by keeping the owner busy talking in the box office and signal to them to get down on all fours and creep past, They were nearly all friends of mine and never failed to greet me if they were in from the country, great lads all of them.

Football

I joined the Knights of Malta about this time. They are a first aid organisation not unlike the Red Cross. We wore a smart uniform and we marched in the annual parade on Saint Patrick's day. We also attended sporting events but were rarely called on to render first aid - the uniform never failed to impress the girls though. I played soccer that winter and paid for my sins by suffering a period of suspension from the Gaelic Athletic Association who controlled both Gaelic football and hurling. As I mentioned in an earlier page it was considered to be against the national ideal to play those foreign games. I found it strange on the soccer pitch not being allowed to handle the ball so I elected to play in goal, and so began my career as a goalkeeper. I was reinstated shortly after the soccer season ended, and to my delight I was picked for the county to play against Mayo in an Irish Press shield match. We won, and I will never forget until the day I die the thrill of walking out on the same team as the greatest Gaelic footballer ever Sean Purcell, and his partner in crime, peerless Frankie Stockwell. Fifty years on from that day it is still fresh in my memory, and Frank's record score of twelve points in the 1956 all Ireland final still remains unbeaten - it is still in the Guinness Book of Records. Galway won and I listened to the broadcast in a foreign city.

I played in goal for the Galway team on Ascension Thursday in 1953 against Meath in Moate. I am not sure after all those years, but if my memory is correct it was the opening of the new Gaelic grounds. Meath had been All Ireland champions in 1949, and they fielded the same team that day. We lost when Paddy Meagen scored a last minute point for Meath, but what remains fresh in my memory and always will was having my hand shaken by Christo Hand, Paddy Tuam Meagen, Paddy O'Brien and the many great stars of that Meath team. I am not ashamed to say that on that day I had my best game ever in the maroon and white of my native county. Kevin Smith the great Meath goalkeeper told me that I was unlucky to be a Galway man, because the greatest goalkeeper in all of Ireland was the great Jack Mangan of Galway. I still consider it a greater honour to be reserve to Jack than to be first choice keeper for another county. Jack went on to captain Galway when they won the All Ireland, a fitting tribute to the man I consider to be the best ever. I truly believe that had he chosen to play soccer he would have worn the green of Ireland.

Under 18 rugby team (second from right back row, brother John fourth from right.) 1950

We reached the Connacht junior final only to lose to Mayo, who went on to win the all Ireland. Despite this I was reserve to Mangan on the senior team but we were beaten by Roscommon in Tuam. However some of the friends I made through playing football are still friends, among them Jack Mahon who starred on the '56 team and on many Connacht teams over the years. I am sad to say that I had taken the emigrant boat long before the long overdue victory in fifty-six. I met Jack at Saint Andrews golf club many years later and we had a great chat about the old days.

His first book "Twelve Glorious Years" was ready for the publishers, and he presented me with a copy. I was honoured to see that he gave me a mention.

Boxing

The football season had ended without any silver won but I had enjoyed the experience of playing with some of the greats, something I had only dreamed of as a boy. I was working hard at my trade and training hard for the boxing championships in the evenings. I was determined to win this time and I was going to fight as a light heavy weight. I thought "I will let the others worry about me, they will remember how I was cheated out of the heavyweight title last year and it may be to my advantage". I thought I was lucky to get the decision over Jimmy Moylet in the semi final, but I was due a bit of good fortune as I took a well earned rest before going in to the ring to fight Sergeant Moore in the final.

I found the final was surprisingly easy compared to the semi final, but anything had to be easier than fighting Moylet, a gentleman outside the ring, a tiger in it. I won by a knockout early in the second round, and was greeted at the ringside by the boy who had hammered me in St Joseph's a few years before; he only weighed eight stone and had not grown much. I was very proud when Sergeant Mick Brennan my old trainer from the school came up to me and shook my hand - that was the icing on the cake.

I was matched with Sean Thornton of the Galway boxing club shortly after my championship victory and I fought him again two weeks later losing two bruising battles on points. I was a bit ambitious taking on Thornton who had fought the European heavyweight champion and went down fighting, he was a real fighting Irishman and more than two stone heavier than I was. I should have known better.

S JOYCE TUAM BOXING CLUB

CONNACHT LT HEAVYWEIGHT CHAMPION ✿ 1952-3 ✿

S JOYCE

A Day at the Races

The town closed down on race day every year, except for the pubs that did a roaring trade, and Thady loved to go racing. I was staying at his old cottage that week and I rose early to try and get a lift into town. He asked me to take his bicycle and get some groceries from the local shop, which was about a mile down the road. I was on my return journey travelling fairly fast to save time, when I suddenly found myself flat on my back on the road with the bike on top of me. I found that the saddle support bar had rusted at the bottom behind the metal ring that carried the pump, causing it to snap, and the saddle shot backwards throwing me onto the road. I carefully put the two broken ends of the bar together and I slipped the metal ring over the joint, and slowly walked the bike back to the house. I said a hasty goodbye and started off on foot, putting as much distance between Thady and myself as possible. I had only travelled a couple of hundred yards when I heard the roar. Thady in his Sunday best had hopped up on his bike, and the saddle had shot backwards like an ejector seat depositing him on his posterior in the centre of the road. "The curse of Jasus on you, you have wrecked my f*!!ing bike!" I saw him from a distance at the races that day but I made sure to keep well away from him until he had cooled down.

I went down to Lynch's bar that evening as it was his favourite watering hole, and I was surprised to see the bike outside the door. I met one of the local lads and he laughingly asked "What did you do to Thady?" I explained as best I could and said I could not understand how he had ridden the bike to town. "No problem", he said, "he removed the saddle, pushed the brush handle down the pipe, put the saddle back and off to the races."

If there was a football match in the town Thady would call at the house for his dinner - my dad insisted on this, much to the annoyance of my stepmother. The only people who could do no wrong in her eyes were the clergy, everyone else she never failed to find fault with, especially her brother. She would get very annoyed if he decided to ride out to Gill's pub for a few pints, and one Sunday he asked my brother to accompany him. He always boasted that it was impossible to get him drunk, but he was ready for lift off after two pints of Guinness. One Sunday as they were on their return journey they were cycling down Quinn's hill about two miles from the town when my brother saw a cow lying in the centre of the road. Thady had a fairly new racing cycle, and how he acquired it is a funny story but it would take too long to tell - anyway he raced down the hill like a bat out of hell. My brother waited for him to slow down and make his way around the cow, but to his horror he drove straight at her, hit her amidships and sailed over the handlebars to land on the broad of his back on her other side. The poor animal nearly died of fright and bolted as my brother ran over to pick up the corpse of poor Thady. He had not allowed for the staying power of the bold Thady however - he jumped up and shouted, "Did you see that stupid bitch run out in front of me?" He shouted a few obscenities after the terrified beast, said "take my bike to the repairer" jumped on my brother's bicycle and sped away. He was seventy-five years old at that time, had smoked from the age of six, and drank Guinness by the gallon all his life - what a man.

I remember many funny happenings that occurred during the time I knew Thady, but one really stands out. He decided to enter his twenty-year-old mare in the Milltown races, and he decided that I would be the jockey. I pointed out that I weighed twelve stone seven, that the mare was twenty years old and I had never been on a horse in my life. He gave a knowing smile and said the other owners don't know that, and I wondered what advantage that was to us, but he was not worried. He said "I know my mare and she has great stamina", and I told him that was true but I dared not mention that she had proved it by pulling a plough for more than twelve years. He smiled and said to stay with the bunch for the first mile, then give her her head and she would win easily. We arrived in Milltown and I was decked out in Thady's racing silks an old pair of jeans with the bottoms tucked into my old football socks. I wore a white shirt with my father's old cap turned back to front to complete the picture. The other owners led in their horses and Thady, not to be outdone, did likewise. He shouted at the local bookie to enquire about what odds he was prepared to give and the bookie smiled when he looked at the old mare and saw who the jockey was. "Forty to one", he answered with a twinkle in his eye, and Thady replied "one pound to win the Tullinadaly Lass" "Right you are on", said Honest Joe.

They called us in and the other jockeys dressed in correct attire lined up. The starter dropped the flag and the Tullinadaly Lass turned her back. Thady was armed with a big shillelagh, and he gave her a mighty crack and she broke in to a gentle trot. The rest were out of sight by now and the day was lost. We completed one lap of the track amid whistles and hoots of laughter from the lads who knew Thady and myself. It was all good fun but Thady was not amused. "That is the last you will ride for this stable", he shouted. I believe the craic was great in Lynch's bar the following Sunday. "Why didn't you get Pat Taffe himself down to ride for you, Thady?" they asked, and a pound would buy a hell of a lot of Guinness at that time and a much better return could be had for his pound. So ended my racing career - short and sweet like Thady's mare's gallop.

CHAPTER 9

Leaving Ireland

My stepmother was getting impossible to live with, and she would often disappear for up to two weeks without any explanation and not speak to any of us for a couple of weeks after her return, and I was spending less and less time in the house. We were all unhappy with her, and Thady said she would drive a man to drink. I knew what he meant but I was determined that she would not drive me to drink. Money was scarce even though I was probably earning more than most of my mates, and to make matters worse I got sacked from my dance hall job when the owner complained that I was spending too much time on the dance floor, and he would not be requiring my services anymore. I think he saw no reason to employ me when there was never any trouble in the hall. The following Sunday night his wife's brother was on the door and he must have thought to keep the money in the family. I went to the dance the next Sunday night and paid to go in. At about ten o'clock a fight broke out. The doorman rushed in and got flattened right away, and the owner came over and begged me to help. I pointed out that I had paid to come in and that I had been sacked, and said I was not interested. He called at our house next day and said "Will you come back Steve, please?" My replacement had packed in his job on his first night's duty when he got his nose broken. "I will pay you an extra ten shillings to come back", he said, but I replied "Two pounds a night or I am not interested". He reluctantly agreed - he was making a fortune yet he begrudged paying me a pound and now he was paying me two pounds because of his greed. There was no trouble after that. Today the dance hall is a hospital.

The music they play on Radio Eireann is not the stuff they played when I was a boy and it appears to me that anything Irish is not in fashion. Most of the popular Irish groups adopt a nasal American twang, something I love to hear if an American is singing, but it sounds ridiculous and phoney when copied by a person who is not American. Much of today's music is called Country and Irish - who ever heard such nonsense. All Irish music is country music. Irish railroad workers took their music with them to the States, and we are now buying back what we gave away for nothing. I find it very strange that one can hear top Irish bands in Britain or America nearly all year round, where there are lucrative circuits to keep them occupied, while you would have great difficulty finding one at home.

I must confess that a lot of people leave Ireland who have no need to, and I was probably one of these. I was very unhappy at home through no fault of my father and I was getting restless. I got a shock a few weeks later when my employer called me one morning and said, "I am very worried Steve, there has been a big drop off in business, and if it continues I may have to close". Apparently a new shop had opened in town and was selling cheap sub-standard furniture at a fraction of our prices, and though it looked good it was anything but. My employer, a man with a great reputation, would not lower his standards, and his worst fears were realised a few weeks later when he sadly said "it is no good Steve, we cannot compete" and said he would have to close.

I was upset for him because he was forced to close a business that was started by his grandfather, and must have been worried about his family's future. I was only young and I had no ties, and like a lot of my countrymen I was getting a touch of the wanderlust, and thought I might go to England for a while before deciding what to do with my life. Later that week I met my old teacher Mr Murphy and he said, "I believe your boss has closed the business", and he remarked that the people of Tuam would regret the day they allowed this to happen. He then enquired if I had made any plans, and I said I had not yet made up my mind but I might go to England until Christmas. He said "Why don't you join the Police Force, they are on the lookout for likely recruits". He said "I will talk to a friend of mine in the Force and ask his advice and I will talk to you later". I had a visit from a garda a few days later and he told me I would be a fool not to join, he said "you will most likely be stationed at the depot in Dublin, they have a good boxing team and a good football team and your future is assured". I am sure now as I look back that it was good advice. I made up my mind to go to England until Christmas and then I would apply to join the boys in blue. I did not realise then that nothing is as cut and dried as it looks and that St Joseph's would haunt me for the rest of my life.

I decided to spend a few days helping Thady with the harvest before I left as he was getting old and tired, and we were very close and I knew that I would miss my old friend. Both our eyes filled up as I bade him goodbye and I said "Christmas will be here soon and I will see you then".

I was talking to a friend of mine, who had played rugby for Tuam with me, and he told me a pal of his who was a carpenter was working in England and he was home on holiday at present. He said, "I will talk to him if you like, and he is a great lad and may be able to fix you up with a job". And there a friendship started that is still going strong nearly fifty years on. I was indeed fortunate to meet Martin Higgins, a first class tradesman who not only got me a job but also taught me a lot. On the train to Dublin I was very excited and looking forward to my big adventure, and I was introduced to the young lady who was to become Martin's wife, and she was returning to Manchester with her brother from a holiday in Ireland.

First Steps in England

We arrived in Manchester in the early hours of an August morning, and I was shocked to see how dirty everything looked. The station was very black and sooty and the buildings were the same. I smiled and said 'good morning' to a few people but I soon gave up as they gave me queer looks and never answered me, I wondered if they could not understand my Galway brogue, but I found out later that this was not the case. I was in a big city and everyone seemed to be in a hurry, and I wondered what the hell I was doing in this strange place. Even on that first morning I could feel the pangs of homesickness, and I missed the green fields and rivers of the quiet Irish countryside and the friendly smiles of my neighbours. This feeling has never gone away and remains with me to the present day. The accents of the people too I found strange and everyone was in a hurry, and I found it all difficult to understand. It took me a long time to adjust.

My companion Martin took me to the home of the O'Briens in Swinton, where I was introduced to his future wife's family, great people steeped in Irish traditions. There I was made welcome by that friendly family, who gave a reluctant exile a home for my short stay in Manchester. They put us up for a few days and refused to take a single penny in payment - wonderful people to whom I will always be grateful. It was time to move on so we took the Durham train and arrived in Billingham on Tees after a long tiring journey, where I had no trouble getting digs at two pounds a week. I cannot remember the good lady's name, but she was kindness itself, and told me her brother was Bishop of York. Martin took me to the building site where he worked and introduced me to his employer, who greeted Martin more like a friend than an employer. Martin said, "This is Jack Lamb", and Martin then said to Jack "This is

Steve, will you fix him up with a job?" to which Jack replied, "No problem, when do you want to start?" I had never met a nicer man, and I could not believe how well the English treated our people. It would have shocked the older Tuam people whose only memory of the English was of the hated Black and Tans. I soon came to find that there is a certain bond of friendship that unites construction workers the world over whatever their race, and the Irish and the locals got on very well socially as well as at work. In fact it was not unusual to hear locals invite their Irish workmates to their homes.

Jack Lamb was a big improvement on the Tuam daily mass-goer that rushed home from church to abuse his unfortunate workers.   I started work right away and found the work a lot easier than I was used to. I did not find it any less demanding or less skilled, but I was not harassed or shouted at by a religious nut, and my fellow workers were very pleasant people. I felt like a millionaire on Friday evening as I caught a bus to Stockton on Tees to go to a dance. My bonus for my first week's work equalled my week's wages in Ireland, and after paying tax on an emergency code I drew over twenty pounds.   It felt very strange walking in to the dance hall, which was a much posher place than the Phoenix in Tuam, and not knowing anyone added to my discomfort.   I finally picked up courage and asked a girl to dance, and when the dance ended she introduced me to her friends. They soon put me at ease and in a short time I was made to feel one of the gang.   I explained that I was newly arrived from Ireland, and that my workmates went to the pub on Friday nights and this did not appeal to me. I really enjoyed the evening and arranged to meet them all on the next Friday night. I thought their accents very funny but they were friendly people, and I caught the bus back to Billingham feeling that England was not such a bad place after all.

I was still very homesick but two of the landlady's neighbours talked me into going to an Old Time dance with them the following Tuesday in Billingham, and I found it very strange. They played a dance called The Pride of Erin, and my immediate thought was as a son of Erin, that no one in Erin ever heard that one. I thought the English a very strange race when the singer with the band sang 'Dear Old Donegal' a bloody sight better than I had ever heard it sung in Ireland.

The weeks passed and I looked forward to my Friday nights, which were the highlight of my entertainment. I was even getting to understand the lingo of the locals or Geordies as they called themselves, a friendly people who seemed to have a lot of time for the Irish. One day I arrived home from work to find that the landlady was not at home, and as I had forgotten my key I decided to climb the drainpipe and let myself in by my bedroom window which was at the rear of the house. To my surprise a few minutes later when I answered a knock on the front door, I found the house surrounded by police. Some public-minded person, seeing what they took to be a burglar breaking in, had called the local police station - a strange Country indeed I had never seen an English policeman before and I thought their helmets funny. I thought they were not very practical but they probably made the police look bigger, and might act as a deterrent to would-be criminals.

I used to feel pretty lonely on Sundays probably because I was not working and had more time to think; anyhow I was feeling pretty low as I walked around Stockton one Sunday. I knew the All Ireland hurling semi-final was being played in Croke Park Dublin, and that Galway were playing Kilkenny and I had followed the fortunes or misfortunes if you like of the Galway team over the years. They were always a point in front until the last minutes, yet they always ended up losing by a point - I hoped today would be different. I wondered how they were going on, when I heard the golden voice of Michael O'Hehir booming out from a radio in a house nearby, and I knocked on the door and asked if I might listen to the broadcast. That day I listened to Galway beat Kilkenny, and I wished I was back home to join in the celebrations but I was a very long way from home. They went on to narrowly lose the final to a great Cork team but I was very proud of them just the same. I was to wait another thirty years before Galway would capture the coveted McCarthy Cup.

Manchester Calling

I did not know that my friend Martin and Bridget O'Brien, the girl I had seen on the boat to England were serious about each other, until he told me one day that he was moving to Manchester. I thought that I too would return as I had been told before leaving home that there were some good Gaelic football teams in Manchester. I missed my football and hoped I could find a team in Manchester to play for. I was sad to say goodbye to my new friends at the dance in Stockton on Friday night, and next day we took the train to the rainy city as Manchester is sometimes unfairly called (I consider the south of England to be at least as wet!)

I soon found out that Martin was held in high esteem in Manchester when he called to see the boss of a large company and we were given jobs right away. I got to know my way around Manchester and found my way to the Astoria Ballroom on Saturday night, where I was introduced to a Kildare man called Joe Cahill who ran the Oisins Gaelic football team. Joe signed me on right away and I was fortunate indeed to join the most famous team in Lancashire. This was the team that the great Roscommon footballer Eamonn Boland, winner of two All Ireland medals, played for. I felt honoured to be asked to play for them. In Irish circles in the city I soon found out that news travels fast, as I was approached by two other teams that night and asked to join them.

The Astoria was where our people congregated every weekend, and our people were very supportive of each other at that time. And if a man was looking for a job there was always someone there to offer advice and help. I started to play football again and I was fortunate enough to win two Lancashire championships with

Oisins, and to represent Lancashire County. I did however notice that the standard of fitness dropped considerably when a player moves to another country, and a drop in the standard of play follows. I believe that this is inevitable in an amateur sport when an athlete has to work for a living and cannot afford to get injured. For a start he misses the security of his own home and is paying for his board, but with the security of his family around him he can reach a much better level of fitness. This was very obvious to me when I played in England with and against people I had seen play at home, and I could not believe they were the same players. It was obvious to me too that I was never the footballer in England that I was at home. Professionals do not suffer from this handicap and often improve their performance when they change clubs.

We played a lot of our games at the old White City stadium in Manchester, and Harris Stadium owned by Reg Harris, Manchester's world Cycle champion. Both of those great arenas are gone now and I doubt if we will see their like's again, athletic clubs in and around Manchester are poorer for their going. Reg Harris is also gone and his famous stadium has become part of Manchester University complex. The city lost one of its great sporting heroes when Reg died a few years ago, and I very much doubt if many remember him because you never hear his name mentioned any more, which only goes to show how fleeting fame is. The people involved in Gaelic sport in the city certainly miss the

Stadium, and have never found an adequate replacement.

Home for Christmas

The contract where Martin and I were employed was nearly finished, but I was not unduly bothered as I was returning home for good at Christmas, and I knew Martin would have no problem getting another job. I was saying farewell to Manchester forever, I thought as I took the Holyhead train a few days before Christmas, eagerly looking forward to seeing my family again. I remember the festive spirit was much in evidence as we all joined in a singsong all the way to Holyhead. I don't believe any race on Earth knows how to enjoy the craic like the Irish, and it was one big party all the way. I could not wait to meet my pals again to take up where I had left off. I missed the boxing club and the football, especially the football as I was determined to fight to regain my place on the County panel.

I arrived in Tuam where Dad met me at the station, and I now saw my hometown and I realised just how much I had missed it. I will never forget the excitement of the place. There were farmers, some slightly the worse for drink, selling turkeys and geese and the Christmas spirit was everywhere. I do not know if it is like that anymore, but those are the memories of Tuam that I cherish. People kept coming up to me shaking my hand and saying "Welcome Home" and it made me almost feel that it was worth going away. What a lovely feeling. If people could maintain this goodwill throughout the year what a lovely place the world would be to live in. Alas this cannot be and as soon as the Christmas season ends the other side of man's nature asserts itself.

My stepmother seemed quite pleased to see me, but I was able to detect an uncomfortable feeling about the place where everyone was putting on an act to put me at ease. I made up my mind that if I were going to join the Gardai it would have to be now or never. I decided to return to Manchester for a few months and when I came home in summer I would apply to join the boys in blue. On my return to Manchester I talked to Sean an ex member from Dublin, and I was advised not to leave it too long. He had resigned a few months back and had decided to travel and see the world while he was young, and took the building job to earn some money. He told me I was doing the right thing, and said, "it is a great career and a good pension when you retire". I casually mentioned St Joseph's and he told me to forget about the police force, saying, "you will be turned down when they check up on your background". He assured me that an ex Industrial School inmate would not stand a chance. I thought of my family and the shame a refusal would bring to all of us and asked if he was sure that it was so, and his reply left me in no doubt. I spent a few sleepless nights and finally decided that St Joseph's and the system had won. I would be an Industrial Schoolboy as long as I lived. I decided to return to my trade and make my way in life as best I could. Little did I think that fifty years would pass without spending another Christmas in my hometown.

Nottingham

Martin suggested that we should go to Nottingham as there was a big contract opening up at Castle Donnington, where they were going to build what was probably the biggest Power Station in Europe. He said there would be big money to be made, so once again this lovely man took me under his wing and got me another job. I do not know what I would have done without his help, and we continued to work together until he returned to Manchester some time later to marry Bridget O'Brien.

That year a team of Geordies who worked on the Power Station entered the district football league, and as they had won the league in the town where they had previously worked they were made to play in the first division. I was invited to play for them and as I mentioned early on I got on well with people from County Durham. We had a great season winning the district cup, and I was invited to Derby County for a trial. Harry Storey was the Derby manager at that time and though I thought I had played well, nothing came of it. I was probably earning more money at that time anyhow as professional footballers were only making fifteen pounds a week in those days, long before the minimum wage was brought in and some very ordinary players get more money than a Prime Minister.

We were given a weekend off with pay every six weeks to visit our homes, and I listed Manchester to qualify for the weekend for which we were paid. A pal of mine who was engaged to be married got involved in a gambling card game on Friday and lost all his money. His young lady was looking forward to seeing him and he was at his wits' end as to what he should do. In those days you could buy a platform ticket for two pence and it allowed you access to the platform to greet friends arriving on the train. My pal suggested that we should buy a two-penny ticket and he would travel free by hiding under the seat. The trains were troop carriers with wooden lath seats and he suggested that I should spread my overcoat on top of the seat and he would lie on his back under it. We would repeat the same procedure at Manchester when I would leave the platform and buy two two-penny tickets and return to the train for him and I readily agreed. I bought two singles to Manchester unknown to him and helped him to settle in the cobwebs under the seat. I had difficulty keeping a straight face when the Inspector asked for my ticket and I handed him the two singles, and he enquired whom the second ticket was for. I said it belongs to the gentleman under the seat, he prefers to travel that way. The Inspector must have thought we were stone mad when my companion emerged from under the seat swearing and spitting out spiders. My pal told the Inspector we were going to my parents wedding, but he saw the humour of it when he cooled down. It taught him to keep away from card schools after that.

The football season had finished and I was getting itchy feet, so I thought I might as well return to my adopted home city of Manchester. I arrived there in the late spring and I decided to call and see Martin Higgins and his wife Bridget who had settled down and purchased a grocery business in Harpurhey. Martin was working near his new home on a housing estate that had just started, and once again he found a job for me working with him. I have made many friends down the years, but I have never met a better one or one to whom I feel more indebted.

A Summer with Thady

I decided to go home that summer and I would spend a little time helping Thady on the farm. I had missed the old boy a lot and I knew I would receive a royal welcome from him. I spent a little time at home and then went to stay with Thady, where I went close to losing my life. I had often heard the old people say that it was unlucky to shoot hares, and I had always laughed at what I called silly superstitions. I certainly would not argue with that now, and what happened to me certainly gave me food for thought.

I borrowed a neighbour's gun and I must have shot about a dozen hares that were eating the wheat crop, when I heard a loud bang and I was on the ground. I do not recall falling but I probably passed out for a few seconds. Thady heard the noise and must have thought that another hare had bit the dust and came over to find out, but I was fortunate that he did, for it was me and not a hare that had gone down. He did not panic but hailed a passing priest who administered the last rites, and got someone to call a doctor. His quick action saved my life, without a doubt, as I would surely have died from loss of blood had the doctor not arrived quickly. A local man, who had spent some years working in an English hospital, drove like a formula one driver to cover twenty-two miles in as many minutes to get me to the Galway hospital. When Dr Fitzgerald (for that was the good doctor's name) got to Galway hospital there had been a violent thunderstorm causing a total power failure, and they had to switch on the emergency generator. I was very fortunate to be in the capable hands of a brilliant young surgeon from Tuam named McHugh who most certainly saved my life.

Tuam town will always be listed as the birthplace of two of the greatest Gaelic footballers ever, Purcell and Stockwell. I in gratitude would like to add another great man to the list and he is called Tom McHugh. The great man called to see me the day after my operation to see how I was progressing, and he said, "I am afraid I had to remove your spleen but there is no reason why you should not make a complete recovery, but you will never box again". I was delighted to know that I would make a good recovery, but my secret ambition to box as a professional was over. I had only told a few close friends about it, but I had trained with the professionals and found I could easily hold my own without being fully fit. I must admit they were not top class pros, but they all made a good living.

Return to Britain

When I look back now I realise how stupid I was to sign my release from the hospital, and walk into my home without any warning. I think dad thought I was a ghost. I got stronger by the day however and I decided to return to Manchester and work, rather than my stepmother's tender care. When I returned to work the site agent said "I was told you were dead", and when I assured him that I was not, he said "I am afraid I have a problem, I gave your job to another man when I was told you were dead and I cannot sack him now".

I had had a good job as a charge hand carpenter prior to my accident, but I agreed to work for less money until I found a better job. I did not have to wait long to get a well-paid job. I worked nights building the new Granada Studios in Manchester, in what then was known as a " Pea Souper fog" and the shifts lasted twelve hours. The money was the best I had ever earned, but at that time Manchester must have been the unhealthiest City in the world with thousands of its citizens suffering from bronchitis, and I was determined to get away as soon as possible.

It was hard work and I could not understand the mentality of some of my fellow countrymen who worked so hard, only to blow all their money on drink and gambling. They seemed to be going nowhere at all, and often looking for a sub on next week's wages on Monday morning. Some of the Irish lads had not been home ever since they left Ireland, and though they always talked of going home it was always going to be next year, which meant never because they never had enough money. They were sad men who lacked ambition and lived from week to week.

I was unhappy living in Manchester's unhealthy air, so I was pleased when the company asked me to move to Rhyl in north Wales, where they were building a new Woolworth's shop. It was right on the sea front, and I felt it was just what I needed to recover my strength after my accident. I spoke to a firearms expert who was stationed in Rhyl in the British Army about my accident, which up until now no one could explain; the cartridges had exploded in my pocket, which in theory at least was impossible. The soldier was in no doubt that the accident was caused by faulty cordite packing. I, of course, was not in a position to lodge a claim for damages. Had I been a member of a gun club or if I was someone in authority I am sure a claim could have been made, but sadly I was not in a financial position to do so. Money can ease many problems. I really enjoyed my time in Wales though they treated me very coolly when I first arrived, they explained later that they thought I was English until they heard me speak. There are times when it pays to be Irish.

I went to Cardiff Arms Park to see Wales play Scotland at rugby, and watched the great Cliff Morgan lead Wales to victory. It was a great atmosphere but not nearly as exciting as Croke Park on All Ireland day, but that applies to any other sporting event on earth. Yes, Croke Park is unique. The seaside air was a big change from the Manchester smog, as Mancunians called it, and I soon began to return to fitness. I knew that I would never again be as fit as of old, but I was much better than I ever expected to be, and I liked Rhyl, a friendly town. There is always something or somebody to put a fly in the ointment, and from day one this was in the shape of a five foot three little swine from Liverpool who hated all Irishmen. How he got to be foreman carpenter will remain a mystery to me, though the site agent, a big Scotsman, assured me that he had not promoted him.

Mr McKaskey told me that he was married to a sister of the company secretary, and assured me that he was not qualified to work as a carpenter, so he always found fault with other people's work. I took an instant dislike to him and the feeling was mutual, and I am not proud to say that some of my fellow countrymen did everything but crawl to please him. Like some small men he loved to lord it over big men, and he loved 'pulling rank' as the locals called his bully-boy ways. He made the mistake of trying it on with me one day, and I left him in no doubt about what would happen if it continued. He left me alone after that but there was an unpleasant atmosphere about the place, and I had seen enough bullying in St Joseph's to last me a lifetime. I vowed that never again would I let anyone push me around, and I have kept that vow. Mr McKaskey knew that I was unhappy there and said "I will try to arrange a transfer for you as soon as possible," and he was as good as his word. What really got under my skin was when some of those creeps came up to me to say "fair play to you" when I told him to make sure he attended his parents' wedding as I was leaving. It takes all sorts.

I returned to Lancashire and got digs right away and started work on Bury General Hospital, and it was a pleasure to work with normal human beings again. I liked the countryside around Bury as there were many farms in the area to remind me of home, and my fellow workers did everything to help me settle in my new job. We spend most of our waking hours at work so it is important that we try to be happy in the work place, and I found a much friendlier crowd of people there. The working day seemed to pass quickly and we seemed to get more work done, even though there was no harassment or unpleasantness.

I took a special interest in the farming methods of the locals who seemed to have a machine to carry out even minor tasks. I was struck by the neatness of the fencing around the fields, and how they were all tilled up to the boundary fence. This was in complete contrast to home, where most fields seemed to have a margin about ten yards wide, totally overgrown with weeds around the tilled area. I suppose we have so much fertile land in Ireland that it does not matter, though it does seem a sinful waste when we are now importing Dutch potatoes and Cyprus cabbage to the most fertile land on earth. A sad reflection on our people. There was a time when we were regarded as the hardest working race on earth, not so anymore I am afraid. We have now caught what Irishmen used to call the English disease. When I first arrived in Britain if there was a difficult job to be done it was always an Irishman at the helm. This is still the case in many instances but today England is much more cosmopolitan, and today other races are doing jobs that once were only done by the Irish.

My return to Manchester was a time for forging new friendships, when I first met up with a man from our neighbouring County Mayo. We got into conversation after mass one Sunday, and what was meant to be a two-minute chat lasted two hours. We became workmates the following week and we are still best friends over forty years later, and a man with a better sense of humour I have yet to meet. I consider myself fortunate to call Aidan Sloyan my friend.

I worked on the renovations at what used to be the old London Road Station in Manchester many years ago, and decided to carry out a search of the underground rooms I had discovered deep in the bowels of the earth. We had a little foreman with a pronounced six County (Northern Ireland) accent, who placed my work bench half in half out in the winter weather on the end of the platform. The southern Irishmen who made up the greater number of the work force, assumed that he kicked with a different foot to us. Whether or not this was the case I will never know but he was a little man with a sadistic nature, who tried to make our lives as difficult as he possibly could. I remember it well as it was an exceptionally bitter cold winter and the little foreman was one of the meanest people I ever encountered.

Making sure he was well out of the way I set out on my voyage of discovery. I was about to return having found only cobwebs, when I saw what looked like a wooden barrel in the light of my torch. On further investigation I uncovered the name Jameson's Irish whiskey under the dust. I planned to return later with a small drill and a wooden plug and a couple of empty bottles just in case. I will never know how it was overlooked, (it was stamped 1916, a significant year in our history). I returned home every day for a full week with two bottles of the best Jameson's ever distilled. I had not made allowance for the little 'Wee Mon' however and he followed me and discovered my secret. He then declared the underground out of bounds, and from then on it was to all but the Wee Mon, until one day he got so drunk that he drove the tractor off the edge of the platform and almost killed himself. He was dismissed for being drunk at work, so life became more pleasant for everyone and some good came of it. 1916 was not a bad year after all.

CHAPTER 10

Life Gets Sweeter

Not long after by a stroke of good fortune I was lucky enough to meet the young lady who would become my wife. One Sunday just as mass ended I was approached by a father Murphy who was a curate at St Edmunds my local parish church. My first thought was another ticket seller and he said "I suppose you will be taking part in the Whit Friday walks," and I assured him that I would, and he then persuaded me to buy a ticket for the church dance. I bought a ticket but I had no intention of going to the dance, as church dances were notoriously dull affairs and after the previous year's flop I said never again.

The Manchester Whit Walks were special and I believe unequalled anywhere on earth, when every one of the many catholic parishes in and around the City marched. It was a blaze of colour, and some very famous bands marched, notably The Kerry Pipers and the Terence McSweeneys, and when they marched listening to them play 'The Wearing Of The Green' made you feel like you were back home in Ireland. My lasting memory is of a giant of a man leading the McSweeney's - sadly he passed away a few years ago and I doubt if we will see his like again. They finished off the day with the massed crowds singing "Faith of Our Fathers" a truly awe-inspiring sight and sound. Sadly those great days are gone forever and the walks no longer take place.

There was a feeling of anti climax when the day ended and I thought, "I might as well go to the dance, I will just put in an appearance and slip away early". That was the luckiest evening of my life - thank you Father Murphy. I did not believe you when you said I would enjoy the annual dance. It was the best dance I ever attended. We arranged to meet later that week and we became almost inseparable, and I realised that I had met the girl I wanted to marry.

Fun and Games

We enjoyed a great social life in those days with a lot of good Irish dance halls to choose from - we were spoiled for choice. I was a bit surprised at the number of English people who attended the Irish halls, and the big Irish dance bands of that era had an enormous following. The first of the show bands The Clipper Carlton could pack any hall in England, and the Johnny Flynn band from Tuam played a lot in Manchester, giving me an opportunity to meet members of the band who were my friends, and indeed the band called at our house often.

Bill Sloyan, a brother of my pal Aidan, opened the Manchester Irish Social Club in partnership with Noel Considine a Cork man, and it flourished for a time. We had some good times there, but Manchester Corporation demolished the building as part of an area clearance scheme and it was a great loss to the local people. Aidan was a great storyteller and could hold a captive audience spellbound everywhere he went. He once told me about a trick he played as a boy. On fair days in his hometown the farmers always parked their donkey carts in the pub yard and late that evening, much the worse for drink, they climbed into their carts knowing that the donkey knew his way home. The bold Aidan changed the donkeys around. You can picture the scene when the farmers rolled up on the wrong side of town in the early hours to be greeted by the very irate wife of another man. As he rightly points out we had to find ways to amuse ourselves in the old days when no one owned a TV and very few homes had a radio.

The Blond Hall in Cheetham Hill was also a popular meeting place for the Irish in those days, and there was dancing there every weekend. It is now the site of the Irish World Heritage Centre, and it must be the finest tribute to our people anywhere. It was built by voluntary labour and has the finest concert hall, conference room and even a restaurant and generally speaking the finest facilities I have seen. The carpets covering the floors depict the national games of Gaelic football, hurling and handball, and it is a glowing tribute to its founder Mike Forde, a nephew of Aiden Sloyan. It even boasts its own drama group and makes one wonder if our exiles show more pride in their national culture than those at home.

I was introduced to a young Welshman born in Cardiff of Cork parents who was a keen rugby player, and he was then going out with a friend of my fiancée Rita. He suggested that I give it a try, and that meeting resulted in my joining his club Heaton Moor and enjoying over twenty seasons playing as a prop forward. I would later on join Rochdale RUFC until I retired from the game. Rugby is a game ideally suited to the Irish temperament, and while it is a game played mostly by the minority especially in the six counties, I am certain that if a greater number of people played the game Ireland would enjoy much more success at International level. The same Welshman had his stag night the night before the annual derby against Wigan. A great relationship existed between the two clubs, and several of the Wigan players attended the stag party. A very close relative of the same Galwayman, being the only sober man in the house, was asked to run six members of the Wigan Rugby Union team to catch the last train home from the stag party. The sober Galwayman played for Rochdale, and by some accident he put the Wigan players on the Glasgow train in Manchester. When they sobered up they found themselves in another country too late to get back in time for the game. Wigan with six reserves were unlucky to lose by twenty seven points next day. Anyone can make a mistake.

On match days at Rochdale Rugby club an elderly gentleman is responsible for heating the water in the communal bath and he is known to all as Jack. Now I am told by some of the older members that he was once known as Jack the lad, and famous for some of the scrapes he got into. In his younger days he was a very good wing three-quarter, and no mean sprinter. One match day his wife had planned to go to a wedding and asked Jack if he could take their three children to the game and he agreed to do so. On his arrival in Yorkshire where they were to play, Jack knocked on a house door near the rugby ground and asked the woman if he could leave the three children while the game was in progress. The kindly lady agreed and Jack got undressed and joined his teammates on the field. It just so happened that Jack played the game of his life that day and he scored three tries, and ended up getting legless drunk. He returned home on the team bus and was asleep in his favourite chair when his wife arrived home and said, "I see you have put the kids to bed". Poor Jack almost sobered up on the spot as the reality of what he had done struck him and he said "My God, I left them in Yorkshire". His wife screamed "My children, what have you done with them?" He then tried to explain that he had left them with a woman near Keighley Rugby club. To cut a long story short the lady in question had contacted the Police earlier, and the oldest child was able to tell them his name and where he lived. Jack was a very relieved man half an hour later when a Police car delivered his family safely at his door, and his hysterical wife returned to normal and decided not to divorce him after all.

Taking the High Road!

On another occasion we had played a game in the Lake District and some players had overindulged themselves on pints of the local brew. There is nothing new about that kind of behaviour in rugby clubs all over the country, but on this occasion I was approached by a young man who had just played his first game for the club and he had scored a try. He had drunk about eight pints when he remembered that he had come in his car and he had brought his girl friend with him. He then decided that as I was the only non-drinker on the team I was the logical choice to drive his car home. I told him that I had planned to take my wife out for a meal that night as I did not fancy driving a two seater with three passengers all the way from the back end of God speed to Rochdale. For a start I did not know the way and the car owner was falling asleep and could not be relied on to direct me. His young lady was close to tears and said "Please help us as I told my parents I was only going to a home game, and he was asked to play here when there was a late cry off, and that is why we came by car". I would not have minded driving his car which was a low slung two seater, but getting a sixteen stone prop forward, a fifteen stone hooker with a girl on his knees into two bucket seats did not appeal to me. I was going to refuse when my mind was made up for me as I saw the taillights of the club bus disappearing around the corner. They had assumed that I had left after failing to find me, so I was left with no choice but to drive the sports car. The owner had by now fallen into a deep drunken sleep in the passenger seat and was in no condition to direct me, and I had no idea of how to find the Motorway. His girl friend said, "I was here once before but it is a while since, but I think if you take a left here it is a straight road home". I did as she directed and soon found that I was headed for Scotland, and I thought, "what have I let myself in for?"

I tried to think of a way out of the mess as I got further away from where I was trying to get to, and I realised that to make a U-turn was against the law. I finally decided that I would have to chance it as I waited to find a good place to turn. When no lights were visible and the centre area was flat I put my foot down and locked hard to the right The little sports car jumped over on to the central reservation and sunk to her axle, and just to add to my woe the engine stalled. In a state of panic I jumped out and tried to push the car. It would not move and the girlfriend burst in to a flood of tears, which only added to my misery. She wailed "My parents will have notified the police that I am missing, as I told them I would be home by six o clock". That was all I needed, as I dragged the drunk from the car and tried with the girl's help to push it on to the Motorway. I have always been known as a strong man but it would not move no matter how I tried. I said a prayer and with a mighty heave I got it over the edge where a passing car just missed hitting it. The young lady was covered in mud up to her knees, and the drunk was asleep in the mud in the centre of the reservation. I half lifted, half dragged him and somehow got him into the passenger seat and his young lady climbed onto his lap. I pressed the starter but it would not start, and I tried again but no luck, so I tried to flag down a passing car. All I got was "Get off the f*****g Motorway you prat and put your f*****g lights on!" Once again I pressed the starter as the battery was dying and God be praised the bloody thing started. I topped the ton as I flew to Rochdale and vowed never to play the Good Samaritan again. How they got home I don't know as he was on a different team the following week, but she was hailing a taxi as I drove away from Rochdale town hall.

A 'Monster' Mistake

The rugby social life was an outstanding feature of the game, and we enjoyed many a good evening in the company of the friends we had made. The highlight of the social calendar was the rugby ball, held in the ballroom of Rochdale town hall. It was customary that the forwards took their turns on the door to repel undesirable gatecrashers. I had consented to do the first hour on the door knowing that this would release me to enjoy the rest of the evening with my wife. I had not been at my post long when I was confronted with a scruffy looking individual with hair down to his waist who insisted he was the bandleader. He looked nothing like the famous Eric Delaney whose band had played for us in previous years. He was not in evening dress and certainly not a rugby playing type.

I informed him that I was "the Pope" before throwing him out. Inside the hall people were getting impatient as the band refused to play without their leader. A search party was formed and you can imagine my embarrassment when the scruffy individual reappeared to beg admittance with the rest of the band. It turned out he was who he said he was -"Screaming Lord Sutch" of the Monster Raving Loony party. A blushing prop forward apologised profusely to his lordship, and I have yet to live it down. Years on and the tale is still told in the bar of Rochdale rugby club and grows in the telling. Oh, the infamy.

Something to get excited about

I have had some great times during my years playing sport, though sadly I never had a chance to advance my career as a Gaelic footballer as I had taken the immigrant boat before I was twenty one. I also had the good fortune to meet a lot of nice people, some of them famous - among them was Peter Lever who played cricket for England on many occasions. Peter was a fast bowler, and he was no slouch when he played on the right wing for Rochdale Rugby Union Club. It was Peter who told me about a famous victory for Ireland when they beat the West Indies who were the World champions at the time- my response was "God help the cricket-playing Nations if we ever take it seriously"!

I could never get excited about the game though I went to watch my son Tim play on a few occasions. (Tim is no mean player as he was captain of the South Lancashire league for a number of years). One incident stands out in my memory when I took Tim to a cup game when he was about fifteen years old, and he was appointed as scorer, in other words he kept the score board marked. There was a great panic when one umpire failed to put in an appearance, and a substitute could not be found. An official told the home captain they would have to forfeit the game if they could not get an umpire in the next ten minutes, and after much pleading I allowed myself in a moment of madness to be talked into doing the job.

To start with I did not know the rules of the game, and I was given a hurried briefing in a language I did not understand by the home club secretary. He told me to look at him if I was unsure of anything and he would indicate what I should do. I went into the dressing room and saw two umpires' coats hanging on pegs. One was a size forty-two chest and the other would have been too big for the great Finn Maccool. I took the smaller coat and managed to squeeze into it. The other umpire who was about eighty years old with a twenty inch chest topped by a size two collar, gave me a dirty look as he wrapped Finn Maccool's coat three times around himself and tied a piece of rope to keep it in place - and we were ready to go.

I took up what I hoped was a correct position and I found myself confronted by a giant West Indian with a lovely musical voice and he asked me for a line. Now in the building trade a line is a piece of string and I looked in vain at the secretary for guidance, but he only gave me a blank stare. I told the batsman he was here to play cricket not to set out a building foundation, and the poor fellow must have thought I was drunk. He took his stance, shook his head and never spoke another word. However he was soon on his way back to the pavilion as I raised my finger to indicate that he was out. I saw the secretary give a faint nod and taking this to be our pre-arranged signal, I raised my finger trying to look as professional as possible as I had seen it done on T.V. The musical voiced one was not amused however, and ranted on about how the standard of umpiring had gone to the dogs. My fellow umpire looked in a state of shock, and I concluded that everyone wanted to bat as fielding involved a lot of running, and they all complained when they were given out.

The visitors were soon all out and I have never witnessed such bad sportsmanship, as they continued to argue with my decisions. One questioned if I was blind, and another told me I needed to read the rule book but I sent him on his way as I was not going to tolerate that sort of talk. To cut a long story short the home team won, though they were complete outsiders, and they all insisted on shaking my hand. I could tell they were delighted at not having to forfeit the game. And grateful that I had consented to umpire it. I did not wait for tea, as I had no desire to sit at table with such bad sportsmen. I was never asked to umpire another game, and I still don't know the rules of that bloody game. Give me a good hurling match any day.

Some Thoughts on being Irish

Having spent many happy years playing rugby, I have never lost my love for Gaelic football. Having seen the facilities available to rugby players I think that Gaelic sport is not catering properly for its members. Every Rugby club has its own clubhouse and a bar where the members can get a drink after a game, and they can hold social functions and dances to bring in more money to help purchase jerseys, footballs, etc. I would like to see our clubs doing this, and as they get much bigger crowds attending their games than the Rugby clubs do they would get enormous support attending social functions. Most players go for a drink after a game anyhow and I am sure they would rather spend their money in their own club.

It may be that familiarity breeds contempt but it is rare to see a Ceilidh advertised in the Ireland of today, whereas you could go to one in Ireland every week in the fifties. Some people will say they are old fashioned, but they are very popular in England and English-born contestants regularly win prizes at Irish dancing competitions in Ireland, and Manchester boasts one of the finest Ceilidh bands anywhere in St Malachys. The American Irish too never forget their roots, and I have heard them express disappointment when visiting our country wishing to attend a Ceilidh, when there is a disco in every Town but it is almost impossible to find a Ceilidh. It is sad to see our culture being so sadly neglected and I cannot help wondering what will happen to it when my generation are gone.

I consider our national games to be at least the equal of rugby and soccer, yet there are greater numbers of Irish following the fortunes of Manchester United and

Liverpool than there are following their county teams. We have lost touch somewhere along the way. Having played all three games, Gaelic football remains my first love. I played soccer for Hyde United in what was then the Cheshire League as a part time professional, but as it entailed two nights training I gave it up. My employers were not impressed by me finishing work early to go training, and the money I received for my endeavours was not enough to justify my carrying on. I enjoyed the experience but in truth I found soccer tame, and I had started to play for Oisins again and I was also playing rugby for Heaton Moor. Then there was the continuous worry about suffering injury, something that was always on my mind especially now that Rita and I were in the process of purchasing our new home, and were soon to be married. I was never completely at ease in my mind on the football field and I always felt that I was holding back, something that never occurred to me in Ireland. I really liked rugby more than soccer and always wished that I could have played before my accident when I was fully fit.

Making Champions

I thought I was too deeply involved with sport already, when I was approached by a young man from Liverpool who worked as a Youth Leader for Manchester education requesting me to start a Boxing Club. I knew that I could not box ever again but boxing was still in my blood, and I said I would give it a go. I never dreamed at that time that we would achieve anything like the measure of success we went on to enjoy. I think that boxing is in every Irishman's blood and I suppose we just love to fight, hence the term the Fighting Irish given to my countrymen many years before I was born.. It is also a title proudly adopted by the famous American Army Regiment "The Fighting Sixty Ninth" and of course the American College football team Notre Dame. We are a nation famed for fighting every ones battles except our own, but as the poet wrote all our wars are merry and all our songs are sad. I think it is time to win something even if it is only a football game.

I knew from day one that Collyhurst - where the club was situated - was a deprived area, famed for having produced Jacky Brown who became flyweight champion of the World. I first made contact with the local schools to see if I got any response, and I was delighted when over twenty boys turned up for training on the very first night. But it was one thing to get boys in to train, and another thing to keep them coming. I need not have worried, for not only did they continue to come but also I got five outstanding prospects in the first bunch. We were on our way and we kept away from all competitions during our first ten months. I was determined to surprise everyone when the schoolboy championships came around. The day finally dawned and we were fairly confident that the boys would not let us down, but it is one thing to look good in the gym and I was worried that they might suffer stage fright, as their opponents were all experienced boxers having had many bouts in public. I need not have worried.

The boxing writer for the Manchester Evening News, John Gaynor, was astonished to see five unknowns pick up four County Champions' medals and one unlucky runner up. John Gaynor was a Dublin man who travelled the Country covering the noble art for the local paper. He was astonished to see a bunch of young unknown boys outclass lads who were hot favourites to capture titles for well-established clubs. Needless to say, the Club leader Peter Coughlan was overjoyed as was the district organiser Mr Green. We went on to produce countless champions, but I will never forget the night I saw one of my boys become Champion of Great Britain, and I watched him repeat his success a year later. Two more of our lads went on to win National Titles, but the unluckiest of all the boys I trained was a lad called Carl Bailey, who won his first forty six contests only to be adjudged a loser in the British Championships. Although he was to win four Northern Counties titles, he never had any luck in his quest for a National Title, yet he went on to enjoy a good career as a professional.

CHAPTER 11

Settling Down

Rita and I got married in October of 1958 and I finally had a home of my own, and for the first time in my life since my mother's death, I knew peace of mind. I was married to someone who knew all about St Joseph's, and was shocked to learn that the Ireland her parents had taught her to love could treat orphans with such cruelty. She had been to a Catholic grammar school and she had always been told that Ireland was the Land of Saints and Scholars, where the Religious Orders were all kind God-fearing people, and when I told her how we had suffered at their hands she was in shock. I still cannot understand why everyone I know has only heard good reports about Religious Orders in Ireland, when so much that has remained hidden is now coming to light. There must have been an awful lot of covering up done.

I was turning out weekly for Heaton Moor rugby club, and as all rugby was played on Saturdays at that time I was also playing for Oisins on Sundays. This was a pretty demanding schedule as I worked until twelve thirty every Saturday, leaving very little time to get to the club especially if we were playing away. Oisins had reached the Lancashire County final due to be played at Harris Stadium and I could feel some of my old eagerness returning, and when my wife Rita presented me with our first child - a boy, John Edmund - I was determined to win it for him. There had to be some problem however and it would have been the first time in my life if things had been straightforward.

Rita had arranged for our son's christening on the following Sunday. It so happened that the Gaelic football final was due to be played on the same day, so we had to go cap in hand to a less than obliging parish priest. He was a very difficult man who seemed to think that he was the most important person in the world, and it is easy to see now why people have turned against the Church, which was always meant to serve the people, and not the other way around. To my delight we not only won but I was fortunate enough to score the winning goal, and it pleased me that Rita's father was present at the final, the first Gaelic football match he had ever seen. I presented my mother in law with my winner's medal later on, and we duly celebrated our son's christening a week later.

CUP WINNERS . . . *Oisín Gaelic football club, Manchester, who won the Lancashire Co. final last Sunday.*

The Oisins team that won the Lancashire cup in 1959. Second from right on the front row is the author, and seventh from the right is Joe Cahill, team captain, with the cup.

A Near Miss

Life was pretty hectic at that time as once again I changed my job to chase better money, and this took me to Halewood in Liverpool to work on the site of the new Ford Motor Company Building where I worked twelve hours a day. The rugby season had finished and there were not many Gaelic football games being played, unlike back home where one could play all year round weather permitting, although the Championships were always played in summer. This gave me an opportunity to work longer hours, and I had an additional source of income as driver of the workers' bus. This involved picking up a busload of men in Manchester at daybreak and arriving at Halewood not later than eight o'clock every morning. I did this job for quite a while but the human body can only take so much, and though I was a strong man I was getting weary of all the travelling. My mind was finally made up for me when an incident occurred which nearly cost me my life. As I was driving the works bus through Salford one evening, I dozed off for what must have been a split second and almost hit an oncoming lorry. I told Rita about the incident when I arrived home and she pleaded with me to change my job, and I gave notice of my plan to leave the company next morning. My employers were very understanding and considerate however and arranged a transfer to Manchester for me right away.

It was nice to be working normal hours again and seeing more of my family. I started working with Aidan Sloyan again as he had continued to work in Manchester during my time in Halewood, and as he was my sons godfather, we had always kept in touch. There was never a dull moment working with Aidan who apart from being a good friend is a very humorous man. He comes of a very talented family, and his sister, who is a renowned artist, was approached to paint Our Lady for the shrine at Knock, and her work is on display there for all to admire. He kept me amused all through the working day but it never stopped him working, and he was always a great favourite with employers and workmates alike.

One of his tales was about an old Scotsman who worked with him when he first came to Britain, who it appears was partial to a drop of a famous Scotch Whisky, and according to Aidan he confused some pet goldfish for herrings one day and fried them for his evening meal. I have been told by many different people that Aidan is a talented singer and sang with a dance band back home as a youth, I believe it is true though I have never heard him sing. I do know that he is a good enough Magician to earn a living on the stage, as I have seen him keep people entertained for hours with an endless line of tricks. There is no end to his talents. I think he has discovered the secret of staying young, as he looks no different today than he did when I first made his acquaintance all those years ago.

Suffer the Little Children

Rita and I were now the proud parents of a second son, Tim, and thought it was time we moved to a larger house. We spent a lot of time driving around the district on Sundays until we finally found just what we were looking for, and we moved to a very nice area convenient for the shops and more importantly our children's schooling, now that John had started school. I was going to make sure that their schooldays were happy and they would carry happy memories with them through life, unlike the nightmares I suffered from time to time and still do.

Later that year while we were on holiday in Ireland I encountered another example of the cruelty that some nuns were capable of. We were coming to the end of a two weeks holiday at home in Ireland when our second son Tim was just fourteen months old, and he was taken sick suddenly one summer's evening. My wife had put him to bed as usual early in the evening and he went to sleep right away. My father looked in a couple of hours later to check that he was all right and was shocked to find the little fellow hanging over the side of his cot gasping for air. He called my wife who called a doctor right away. The doctor quickly examined the little boy and said, "he must be taken to the hospital straight away. I am afraid he is suffering from bronchial pneumonia and his life is in danger."

We were hoping to return to Manchester the next day having enjoyed our stay in Ireland and this came as a terrible shock. We rushed the child to the Bons Secours hospital in Tuam and prayed that he would be spared. On our arrival we were a bit surprised by the curt way the nuns treated us, but we put it down to what we took to be concern for our little boy's health. They dismissed us in a matter of minutes and told us we had better go as we were no use there, and again we thought they were being professional. The child slowly recovered but the nuns got more abrupt and unfriendly as time passed, and my wife, who had been to Notre Dame grammar school in Manchester, was shocked when she was hardly allowed to hold our little boy though he cried for his mother. She left in tears on a few occasions with Tim's cries ringing in her ears, but nothing made any difference to those heartless sisters.

143

I had returned home with our older child as I had to return to work, and my wife's mother looked after John. When they released Tim from the hospital they again acted as though they did not care. I always thought that children's nurses had to have a vocation, as those I have come across in England have always been extra kind to the little ones, but I am sad to say those in the Tuam hospital lived up to what I knew of nuns as a child.

I often wonder if we have sent our best nursing talent overseas, because the people in England who have worked with the Irish nurses cannot speak highly enough of them. Perhaps I have been unlucky in the number of unkind and cruel members of the profession I have met who just happened to come from Ireland, but those from outside the religious orders I have encountered have been normal decent human beings. I have been told by girls who were educated in convent schools and grammar schools that were staffed by nuns that they were told it is sinful to look at your body in a mirror. Now I would like to find out what is sinful about looking in a mirror, because God must have been satisfied with the finished product, and who are the nuns to find fault with his work. I have always thought it would do the nuns a lot of good to spend a couple of years in the real world, away from cloistered walls and see how they would behave if they were exposed to the temptations of the world. I think they might look at the world differently if they had to earn their daily bread. People who avoid the occasions of sin should be less critical of others, and try to be a bit more charitable towards them.

I could never understand why one order of nuns are allowed to call on houses where there are children of school starting age, while the same privilege is denied another order. In effect it allows the Mercy Convent nuns to canvas in order to entice parents to send their children to their school, while the Presentation Convent nuns are denied that right. I do not know who is responsible for this state of affairs, but if only one candidate was allowed to canvas in an election there would be complaints that one party was being given an unfair advantage. It may be a self-imposed rule on the part of the Presentation Order, and if so it hands a definite advantage to the Mercy nuns. I only mention this because I have heard many people complain about injustice, and say that they were unfairly influenced by a visit from the nuns. In a few cases people who had been to the Mercy as children have insisted on sending their own children to the other order of nuns.

A Third Son

We were blessed with a third son Terry, less than two years after Tim was born, and I was totally happy and able to banish all thoughts of the monsters that ruined my formative years from my mind. I could never get rid of the images of Langan, O'Malley and Ryan completely however and I still get flashbacks to those awful days, and I have often re lived them in my sleeping hours, and

I don't expect I will ever be completely free of them. I am certain those words are being echoed by people everywhere, as many thousands of lives were ruined by the Christian Brothers. I know for certain that was not what Brother Ignatius Rice had in mind when he opened the first Christian Brothers school in Waterford in 1802.

Right or Wrong?

My boxing team at this time were proud holders of every major trophy in Lancashire schools boxing, and as a part time employee of The Manchester Education Authority I was paid a generous salary and appointed team manager and trainer of Manchester Boys boxing team. From day one of my career as a boxing coach I tried to pass on what Sergeant Brennan of the Irish Army had instilled in me at St Joseph's all those years ago. There could not have been much wrong with his methods when my team won The Palfrey trophy for being the best team in Lancashire, The Daily Mail trophy for best team in Manchester, which we won five years on the trot, The Temple Summerville trophy best Manchester schoolboy boxer, (Carl Bailey) and The Williams Trophy, for best boxer in Manchester Catholic schools, (again Carl Bailey). I had exceeded my wildest dreams I thought when Mr Alex Adamson the England Team manager came to see me, and offered me the job as coach (trainer) to the English Northern Counties boxing team. He said, "the England job will be yours when Kevin Hickey retires".

I could not believe this was happening to the Industrial School boy, as Alex said "take a few days to think it over and let me know your decision". I talked it over with my wife and explained that it would involve a lot of travelling, and that I would be away from home for long periods, and reluctantly said 'No'. Alex said, "I think you are making a mistake Steve" and perhaps I was, I will never know. Alex Adamson was a life long member of the Arbour Hill club in Dublin, the club that produced among others Mick McKeon who beat the great Randolph Turpin. Alex is now training the Great Boxing Club in the sky. He was a great human being, may he rest in peace.

Shortly after that I called in to see my old friend Chick Gillen who trained the famous Galway Olympic boxing team, (still does) when I was on a visit to Tuam, and he suggested that we arrange a team match between Galway and Manchester. I was all in favour and it duly came to pass. I cannot describe in words the excitement that the proposed visit to Galway generated. There was a buzz about the place as Pete Coughlan our youth Leader got raffles going and we held a boxing tournament to raise funds for the trip to Galway in the Irish Republic. To those youngsters from Collyhurst it was the most exciting thing that they had experienced in their young lives. I knew that they could not all go as it would be a Manchester team that would travel, and though we would provide the bulk of the team some would be disappointed. I did not fancy the job of breaking the bad news to the unlucky ones.

COUNTY CHAMPIONS AT LAST

FIVE schoolboy champions from Blessed John Southworth Roman Catholic Secondary School, brought honour to their school and to Ancoats Lads' Club (where they train), in the Lancashire Schoolboys' Boxing Championships. As the team gaining most points, the five won the Stephenson trophy. (In the centre of the photograph) which they will keep for a year.

The lads have been the runners-up for three consecutive years.

At the moment, according to their trainer Mr Steve, who is justly proud of his team, the club holds the Daily Mail Cup, the challenge trophy for the best schoolboy in Manchester, the Temple-Somerville Trophy and the Williams Trophy for the best in Catholic schools.

The boys will go forward towards the national championships with the exception of Joe Pennington who is only 12 and not allowed to progress any further this year.

Pictured with Mr A. Smith (left) the Ancoats Youth leader, and with trainer Steve Joyce (right) are from the left, the new Lancashire school champion Roy Brady, Carl Bailey, Johnny Johnson, Joe Kelly and Joe Pennington.

Chick was just as busy in Galway getting the show on the road, and as we were breaking new ground by doing something that had not been done before we were a bit on edge and hoping that it would go on as we planned. We got no encouragement from the A. B. A. or the national schools boxing association because of the war going on in the Six Counties in Ireland, or perhaps it was as one of our people suggested because the top brass were not invited. Had we invited them they would have taken over, and it would probably have been like the trip to America when all the teachers went and they left the people who had done all the work -the trainers- at home.

I always felt that the bold Chick put one over on me when Galway won a close match in Manchester, as he told me his team was mostly inexperienced lads and I put a few raw youngsters on our team. I should have known my old pal better, but all is fair in love and war and we levelled the score in Galway. The people in Galway certainly did us proud, and I will always remember those two wonderful occasions, and my many good friends in Galway with affection. On their visit to Manchester Chick and Brother Damien, who assisted in training The Holy Family and Olympic clubs in Galway presented my wife with a beautiful set of Galway China, a gift we will always treasure.

I moved the boxing club to new headquarters at Ancoats Lads Club when the venue became available, and we continued to flourish for the next two years or so. It was hard work spending three nights at the club every week, added to the fact that there were two tournaments a week most weeks during the boxing season. I would pick up the boys at various locations, take them to the tournaments and deliver them home when it was all over, often in the early hours of the morning. I had had enough, and my own sons were growing up so I decided to make a clean break. It was a wrench leaving behind the finest bunch of youngsters I had ever met, I had enjoyed my years in the sport, which I still love and always will, but it was time to go. I handed the boxing club over to a very capable man Johnny Smith, who had trained Alan Tottoh when he represented Britain in the Mexico Olympics. I never go to the fights now because it would not feel the same, though some of the boys still get in touch with me now and again. Carl Bailey who appeared with me on the T.V. programme "Look North" on BBC1 when he had just won his forty sixth bout in an unbeaten run, came all the way from Australia to see me a couple of years ago. I also met another of my star performers, Joe Pennington who was the Northern Counties Champion, a few months ago and he took me to see his Gymnasium which he now owns in Manchester. Joe is carrying on the good work and it would appear that Sergeant Brennan's methods still work. I am very proud of Joe as I am of all my boys as I still call them; they never let me down. They were the best. Most of them are now married with families, but I am sure the days when Collyhurst swept all before them are never far from their minds.

I had tried playing golf on holiday in Ireland but without much success, but now that I had a little time on my hands I booked a few lessons and I joined one of the local clubs. I had met with reasonable success at all the other sports I played, and I was disappointed when it took quite a while before I was playing well enough to enjoy going around the course with my friends. However I became a reasonable golfer in time and even made my club team. I developed a keen interest in the game of golf and I started going to some of the professional tournaments, and through this I met Christy O Connor senior (himself as he is known), and Liam Higgins the Waterville Professional who became a very good friend. Liam, of course, is famous all over the world and one of his feats is recorded in the Guinness Book Of Records. More about the great man later.

St Joseph's Revisited

On a visit to Galway with my wife I decided to call in to St Joseph's, a place never far from my mind, and ask if I might have a copy of my admission form from 1944, and the secretary eventually handed it over, grudgingly I felt. I realised after over thirty years where T. B. Joyce came from, as I was it said T.B. chested. I now knew for certain where O'Malley's cruel taunts came from. I still say that animal was never cut out or fit to be in charge of young orphans that he tortured with his snide remarks. The school as they called it (and I can think of a better name) had changed beyond recognition. The larder where we could on odd occasions steal a loaf was no longer in use, and the big dormitory was divided into small rooms. The Chapel was converted to a Badminton Court and the classrooms were gone. The yard was still there but now silent, but in my mind I could hear Fahy shouting Youls, and the harsh voice of Langan when he knocked a child down with a punch. I did not sleep much that night.

I was pleased to keep in touch with my old teacher Mr O'Donnell down through the years, and I am glad that I took one happy memory away from Brother Ryan's college. His presence in that awful place was the only redeeming feature, and it restored some faith in the human race in the minds of its inmates. I received many letters from him down through the years and when he said on one occasion "We never won the Bishops cup since that day long ago, when yourself and a few others brought it home". I thought, on receiving it, what a miserable life that good man had lived if that small achievement meant so much to him. I can only assume that his life was almost as depressing as ours when he spent his days among so many unhappy people, some of it had to rub off.

One friend of mine, now a prosperous Manchester businessman, who spent four years of his life in the school, still looks back in anger. He was there with his brother for the same reason as me, his father was killed tragically when he was only ten years old, and he still carries the scars from his years of captivity. He suffers from acute depression, and often told me that the shadow of St Joseph's hangs over him still. He said "For some reason I feel guilty though I have done nothing wrong," I suppose being subjected to so much physical and verbal abuse for so many years instils a guilt complex that refuses to go away. I know exactly what he means, and as a fellow sufferer I can sympathise with him. I wonder if the people who inflicted it ever felt any guilt. When one thinks of the countless lives they ruined they must surely have known they were doing wrong. It is to be hoped there will be a day when they will have to render an account. I for one would like to be present.

I thought I might enquire about some of my fellow inmates all those years on, but the secretary was very abrupt and unhelpful, and all I wanted to know was which towns they hailed from, which might have enabled me to make telephone contact. I could not help feeling that she was doing a cover up of some sort, as I cannot imagine any other reason for behaving in such an evasive manner. I have made contact with a handful of the lads over the last forty years, and one in particular had his own dance band in Manchester and it was very popular. Sadly he died last year and is greatly missed on the dance circuit.

I met one other man whom I could vaguely remember and his appearance seemed to contradict his story that he was doing well, I know appearances can be deceptive and I hoped in his case that it was so. Some years ago I ran into a man with whom I had been quite friendly in the school, and I went up to him and said how pleased I was to see him after all those years. To my amazement he pretended not to know me and said he had never heard of St Joseph's, and he knew that I knew that he was lying. I suppose he had his reasons, and perhaps like another man I know he has not told his family of his stay with the holy Monks. I know that it is not something people would want to boast about like a university, but I thought he looked prosperous and I wanted to talk about old times. Perhaps we should wait to be recognised and spoken to before breaking the ice, when we meet an old boy from Ryan's college for young gentlemen. I feel that I have said enough for now about that centre of learning. Anyone one who graduated from St Joseph's learned enough to last him a lifetime.

CHAPTER 12

Nothing Ventured

I always felt that if a man is good enough to make money for an employer then he is surely good enough to work for himself, so I thought it was time to strike out on my own. I decided to give it a try and told myself that the worst thing that could happen would be that I would have to return to working for an employer. To set my plan in motion I decided to contact a large local company and hope that they might allow me to tender for their maintenance contracts. I should have known that there was little or no chance of my being allowed to quote, when I made enquiries and found that a large long established company had done their work for many years.

I still thought nothing ventured nothing gained and went ahead with my plan. I was pleasantly surprised a week later when I received a letter from the area manager asking me to contact him, and I rang his secretary and arranged an appointment. I did not know what to expect when I kept my appointment, and I was a bit disappointed when he offered me some work considered too small to be bothered with by the company doing the maintenance contracts. I decided it would do no harm to get a chance to gain access to the company, and perhaps get to know the people who took decisions.

Making a Name

My first job surprised me as it was on the main roof of a large mill which housed the head area office on the top floor, with the three lower floors stocked from floor to ceiling with goods handled by a large staff. The company was (is) probably the largest mail order Company in the country. I was taken up on to the roof and shown several leaks, and the house maintenance manager told me they had spent thousands of pounds with various contractors without solving the problem. He said, "If by some chance you got lucky and solved this problem, you would get more work than you could handle". I could not believe what I was seeing - the people who had done all the roof work had failed to spot the trouble, which I thought was staring them in the face. They had replaced about a thousand slates when all the leaks were in the valleys, and there were twelve valleys. I nearly laughed out loud but managed to keep a straight face, as I told him I would not only cure the problem but I would be prepared to give a written guarantee on completion of the work.

My biggest problem was not doing the work, but to take more time than was necessary to justify my bill, which I thought in all fairness should be considerable when they had wasted so much with no return for their money. It proved to me that no matter how big the company, they are only as good as the people they employ, and I had laboured hard acquiring what skills I had and they would have to pay for them. I decided to employ a young man who had no knowledge of the building trade but could work to instructions. The valleys were made up of cast iron trays each ten feet long, and the seals were leaking. I had instructed him to clean out all the joints, and I bought a large drum of sealing compound and told him to seal the joints with it. We then replaced all the rusted bolts with new ones. When he had done this I told him to take a long dinner hour and to spend a few days getting a good tan as the weather was warm and the roof was a good suntrap. A week later the weather broke and the manager waited anxiously to see if I had succeeded where the large companies had failed. I knew the roof was watertight and the cure so easy it was laughable, but more importantly for myself I was hailed as the roofing expert and given total responsibility for all roofs on the company's warehouses. I had arrived.

A Funny thing happened ...

I had a young man from south Galway working for me on a large contract which involved spreading a large amount of sealant on a mill roof as part of a waterproofing process. It was a tarry type of bitumen that stuck to everything. On his way home from work he found himself stuck to the bus seat, and had travelled five stops past his stop before he managed to release himself. He visited the home of a friend one night and was shown the new three-piece suite by the man's wife. It had bright orange cushions and she was very proud as she showed it off. Now the lady in question was a very bad tempered person, and as the visitor decided to visit the bathroom he found to his horror on his return that he was stuck to the seat and could not rise without taking the cushion with him. When he finally freed himself by dragging the cushion clear, he turned it upside down, made an excuse and backed to the door. When he got home he was horrified to find half the cushion cover stuck to his behind. He has avoided his ex-friend since that day, and has crossed over the road on several occasions on seeing the man's wife coming towards him, On hearing his tale I remarked that at least the cushions are waterproof.

Losing to Win

The Industrial schoolboy was now a self-employed contractor, if only in a modest way. I could not help wondering what Brother Fahy would have made of it all- he would probably have said that I would go straight to Hell.

I was invited a couple of weeks later to submit an estimate for a large contract, to concrete a large area around one of the companies' warehouses and car parks. I knew that I could not afford to take on the job even if my bid was accepted, as it would involve a large capital outlay and with my limited resources I certainly could not afford it. I went through the normal procedures of measuring up the work to price it, as to admit that I could not afford the capital outlay would ensure that I was finished as far as the company was concerned. There were several others busy measuring the job at the same time as myself on behalf of a number of building firms, and I felt a bit out of my depth in such exalted company, as among them were surveyors and structural engineers.

I decided that if I was to be treated seriously I must tender for the job, so the obvious way to get off the hook would be to work out the most outrageous figure possible and double it. It would then be consigned to the dustbin with the other failed estimates and no harm done. I smiled ruefully as I took a last look at the outrageous figure I had quoted, and thought if this were for real I would be really on my feet, as I sealed the envelope. The closing date was the following week, and I congratulated myself on the clever way I had got out of a difficult situation, knowing that I was off the hook and that I would hear no more about it. I was mistaken though, for I received a letter over a week later informing me that my bid was successful, and that I was a fraction under the biggest local company with my estimate.

Panic stations, what I was going to do. I wracked my brains but the harder I thought about it the more impossible it seemed, until I thought I could only try my bank manager, though I knew what his answer would be. He smilingly invited me in to his office and said, "What can I do for you". I poured out my tale of woe, leaving nothing out, and he looked serious. I had a mortgage and no collateral and when the bank manager smiled I thought he was laughing at me. He suddenly laughed out loud and said, "You deserve to succeed", and enquired about how much I would require. I mentioned a figure much lower than I needed as I lacked the courage to name the proper figure, and he said, "You will need much more than that". He told me I could have the money and said, "We always try to encourage people running small businesses, one day you might be a big business". He then shook my hand and wished me luck.

I got home and as I walked in my wife must have thought I had gone mad as I shouted "I am a millionaire Rita, we are going out to dinner tonight!". I had moved on a bit from twelve shillings a week. I hoped I had not let my Alma mater or Brother Fahy down.

Hungry for Stories

When Christmas came around it was customary for the Mail Order Company to treat all the staff to a Christmas dinner, and on a different day at each mill to enable the kitchen staff to cope, as a large number of meals were involved. Now one man who worked for me had a voracious appetite and made it his duty to find a job that urgently needed doing at the mill where dinner was being served that day. He had eaten five Christmas dinners at the end of the week.

The same man was working with a student I had taken on during the summer holidays, and the young man was driving him mad playing pop music all day on a radio he carried everywhere with him. They were laying concrete one day and the student went for an early lunch to eat before the next delivery was due. To his dismay when he came back, the radio was missing but faint pop music could be heard in the distance. The radio buried under tons of concrete continued to transmit until the battery went dead a couple of days later, and the night watchman refused to go anywhere near that gable, complaining that it was haunted and that he was hearing ghostly voices and music on his rounds.

On another occasion the man with the large appetite was working on a mill roof close to the canal which is nearby. There is an office block in close proximity to the mill, and every lunch time the office manager and his secretary would unlock an enclosed compound surrounded by a brick wall about six feet high, and sit in deck chairs sipping cool drinks. One particularly hot day they locked the compound and went to replenish their drinks. The hungry one was on his lunch break as he gazed longingly at the deck chairs, and without wasting a second he shot down the fire escape, scrambled over the wall and returned to the roof via the inner lift with two deck chairs in tow. There was great excitement when they returned not more than a couple of minutes later to discover that the deck chairs had disappeared, and by now our hero was seated comfortably in a deck chair on the roof, which was out of sight from the compound. I could not condone what he had done, but I am afraid my ribs ached for half an hour afterwards when a search party arrived from the offices to look for the chairs, and by now from the comfort of his deck chair he concentrated on dropping pebbles into the canal to distract a couple of fishermen who were convinced that the fish were jumping all over the place.

Despite all his tricks he was the best worker I ever employed. I had a part time worker, an ex policeman who was working with the hungry one boarding a ceiling one day, and my man hated policemen because he had received a speeding ticket a few months before, and in his mind all policemen were to blame. The floor where they were working was as slippery as glass, and when the ex cop's ladder slipped, he grabbed a red hot pipe to stop himself falling and called his workmate to put the ladder back. He replied that there was a better ladder on the next floor up and he would go and fetch it. The poor man was in agony, as he had to hang on until quite a long time later our friend arrived with the other ladder. "That will teach them not to be so quick issuing speeding tickets", he grinned. Rough justice.

We were concreting a large car park at one of the Companies' mills one day when the firm's netball team who had just won the district league were at practice on the netball court nearby. Now I had subcontracted the job to a local firm and the 'navvies' who worked on the concreting challenged the girls to play them at netball. The challenge was accepted and what followed was not a game for the purists- the 'navvies' played more rugby than netball and I as referee had to abandon the game due to foul play.

I cannot imagine office workers having nearly as many laughs as the building trade workers. I just wonder what the daily mass-goer in Tuam would have made of it all.

I continued to tender for the bigger jobs and I managed to build up a good if modest business, and as my family grew older Rita and myself made sure they enjoyed the little luxuries that were denied their dad. I relived my youth through my boys and got a lot of pleasure out of so doing. I came to love my work, and all Irishmen seem to love the craic, as we call the banter that goes on on the construction sites. One incident keeps coming to mind when my mind goes back over the years. It is of my pal Aidan offering a ten-pound note to a weightlifter who boasted that he could lift double his own weight. All he had to do was place his feet in two large buckets, grip a handle in each hand and lift himself an inch off the ground. Needless to say he failed and the bold Aidan remarked "You cannot even lift yourself". He got his share of muscles, but he was missing the day they gave out the brains.

One thing I became quite good at was pricing work, and I found it much easier to bid against the bigger companies knowing they would be bidding high. They had no choice in this matter because their overheads were so much greater than my own. I started to quote for local council work as my little business grew, and I did housing grant work for Manchester, Oldham, Bury and Tameside Councils. But though I never spent a single penny on advertising, my business, though it remained small, always provided us with a good standard of living. I have seen some people trying to do too much too quickly, and biting off more than they could chew and it goes to prove that it does not pay to be too greedy.

CHAPTER 13

Personal Thoughts

I have been fortunate enough to be able to see parts of the world that were only names on a map when I was young, but I can say in all honesty that the land of my birth is the fairest I have seen, and I have seen many countries - including America. We the Irish owe a dept of gratitude to that wonderful country that gave our people a chance to make a life for themselves in dark days gone by. It is now great to see our economy thriving, and hopefully unemployment and emigration a thing of the past. Every Irish student can now enjoy a college education, something that was only for the wealthy when I was young.

St Joseph's

St Joseph's now houses only a handful of youngsters who go out to college daily and enjoy their lives, but if walls could talk they could tell some awful tales. I wonder if the ghostly echoes of brutal beatings and crying children ever trouble their sleeping hours. I cannot help dwelling on the years I spent in the school, it just will not go away, and I would love to know how it all came to a halt. Did it just close down overnight and if so where did all the boys go, especially if some had no homes to go to? I wonder where the staff went as they could not depend on natural wastage, when there were so many children in their care, someone would have to stay on until the last child left, and I also wonder what brought about the demise of the once revered Christian Brothers. I do not even know if the order is still in being, and if it is, are they still recruiting new members as they must by now have lost all credibility.

Finally did the remaining staff finish up in a home for members of Religious Orders who were retired? I feel that something drastic must have happened for all the Institutions to close in a short time, and I wonder if they found some alternative way to look after orphans and youngsters who committed some minor misdemeanour. I suppose it will all come out one day.

The boys who were there when I last called were older than the senior boys of my time, or so it seemed to me, perhaps they were just better fed, and there were no more than twelve there in total. I cannot see it continuing as the cost of keeping such a large institution open to house a dozen boys is enormous. It could be converted into a hospital or a home for the aged quite easily, and then the ghosts of yesterday might be exorcised. They say time heals everything.

Golf and Society

Though I have enjoyed a decent standard of living and a happy marriage I have always longed to return to Ireland to live. It is not easy, as any exile will confirm, especially when you marry and have a family, or as in my own case grandchildren. A person makes new friends and as is often the case, they become strangers in their hometown due to being so long gone. My modest little business continued to thrive and the worries and pressures of the early days disappeared. For the first time in my life I was able to enjoy foreign holidays, and have a social life. I continued to play golf and became a regular member of the team representing my club in the local league. I played many courses in Ireland, England, Scotland, and Wales, and I was delighted to find no trace of the snobbery that existed in golf clubs in my youth.

When I was a boy only a certain type of person played golf, and they were known as the plus four brigade to us youngsters, and some became members of their local clubs just to mix with people they considered to be the social elite of the town. They were social climbers who looked disdainfully at people who played the native games of hurling and Gaelic football. At that time, the last of those were fading from the scene, as people from all walks of life replaced them in the golf clubs. Golf no longer became the pursuit of people who were members of the professions, as tradesmen and people who would never dream of applying for membership of a golf club in the old days, were not only accepted as members but were welcomed. Today it is standard practise for a farmer or a butcher to make up the Sunday morning four ball with the bank manager and a bookmaker or suchlike.

I was a little surprised to say the least to be asked to become Vice Captain of my club in Manchester after some ten years as a member, and I was pleased to accept. I became captain a year later and the first Irishman to be so honoured. I enjoyed a wonderful memorable year in office, and Rita and I had a hectic social year. It is customary to allow a golf club Captain to play any course anywhere without having to pay a green fee during his year in office, and I had the pleasure of playing most of the best British and Irish Courses during that wonderful year. It is a lovely custom, and the warmth of the greeting and the welcoming handshake you receive as the club secretary puts the clubs facilities at your disposal, is something I personally will never forget.

The Captaincy can be expensive, and a person is expected to perform numerous duties representing his club in his year in office. I have discussed the Captaincy with past Captains and they all thought the year passed too quickly. I could not agree more, and it will always remain a highlight of my sporting life. I am afraid I could not refrain from smiling inwardly as I took my seat in the Captain's chair for the first time, and wondered if Brother Fahy would agree that I was living up to the high ideals he preached about, and doing nothing that might bring disgrace on my old school, that had prepared me so well to face the world. Not bad I thought for one of the Youls. I could not help wondering what O'Malley's reaction would be he had been witness to my first address to the Club membership. He would probably be surprised to see T. B. Joyce was still around. I thought I had finally shaken the dust from The Indust yard from my shoes.

I enjoyed a trip to the golfer's Mecca, namely the old course at St Andrews. It is like Rome to a Catholic or Las Vegas to a gambler, and it is a must for every golfer at least once in a lifetime. I was accompanied by three friends, an Irishman and two English friends, and we were very fortunate with the weather.

The Old Course is difficult enough in mild weather but when the wind blows I am told it can tax the best professionals, never mind the amateur. We were blessed with clear skies and a light breeze and that is how 1 like to remember it, and as you stand on the first tee you feel you are on hallowed ground. I think the ghost of old Tom Morris is still lingering about the place; it has an odd feeling but an enjoyable one.

The Captain's Drive In

TERRY TIM

S. JOYCE
1986/87

I got to know Liam Higgins, the professional from
Waterville Golf Club in County Kerry when he played
the European Tour some years ago.   His reputation
follows him everywhere he goes, as he is one of the
longest hitters of a golf ball on earth and one of nature's
gentlemen.   I have spent many happy hours in his
company, and we were all delighted when he agreed to
come over to play in our Pro Am tournament, and he not
only won but he set a new course record. It was a great
day at the Golf Club, and we finished off the day with a
'hooley' at our house, and quite a number of the club
members getting free golf lessons from Liam in the early
hours of the next day, many the worse for drink.   Liam
then promised to put up a cup to be played for if we
would take a team over to Waterville, and they would

return to play us at Werneth. We did as he requested and were warmly received over in County Kerry, and we enjoyed some great golf on what must be Europe's longest Golf Course. The return match went well also, and started a friendship between the two Clubs which will I hope last forever.

The Werneth golf team: Steve first left on the back row second left is his son, Tim.

I have made many friends in golf as I said before, and Vice Captains' day was a day my family and I will always remember. It was even better on Captain's Final day, and the support I received from the members could not have been bettered if I had been at home in Ireland.

The number of volunteers who gave unselfishly of their time to ensure that my big day went well made me feel that I was really among friends. I hope those customs continue, and bring people together in sport. Sport makes all borders disappear and fosters friendships by bringing people together, and it is something politicians could learn from.

I encouraged my sons to play golf, but only one was bitten by the golf bug, and I am delighted that Tim took a liking for the game. It was a great thrill to play on our victorious team together when we travelled to Waterville, and we have partnered each other to win the Werneth Spoon twice. Our first win with an aggregate score of eighty-four points still stands as the best recorded in the competition. I only mention this to show how things can change in life if you do not give in. Tim is a much better player than I could ever hope to become, and has in fact won practically every competition in the club.

The Future

I think life for my family is far removed from what I experienced as a youth, and I never forget to thank God that it is so. I can only imagine what my fate would have been had I been caught inside the confines of a golf club as a young man with my criminal record. I never committed a criminal act in my life but my record would read I was an Industrial School boy, enough said. I only wish that I had been given the chance to play when I was younger, but I cannot complain as I have had some good times in my life.

Our three sons have done us proud by making a success of their lives, and will never suffer the indignity of being branded a criminal for something they have not done. I, like most Irishmen, miss my homeland, but were I to move home I would surely miss the many good friends I have made in Britain, I think it was an Irishman who said I would like to spend my life travelling if I could borrow another to spend at home.

The changes in Britain are many and varied since I first arrived here as a young man, and I cannot honestly say they have changed for the better. Britain is now a multi cultural State where people from all over the world live and work together. When I first arrived there were very few Asians in Lancashire where today there are large Asian Communities but the same could be said of most European countries. Small communities were broken up when local Councils cleared vast areas, breaking up long established neighbourhoods, when they built high rise flats to house the people. Many families who had lived in an area all their lives suddenly found themselves isolated in strange surroundings, and it became a serious problem for old people as violent drug related crime grew. Burglaries, muggings and robberies became everyday occurrences, and many people were too frightened to leave their homes after dark. Graffiti was never to be seen in the old days, and it was safe to leave your car unlocked at night. Not now I am afraid, and where going to a football game was a great social occasion for all the family, today even the strongest take their life in their hands.

The younger generation is more aggressive than their fathers, and obscene chanting once never heard is now commonplace at games. Something else that strikes me is that stealing tools at work is now taken as one of the perks of the job, and if not locked up at all times they walk. I cannot say if this has happened in Ireland as I only go there on holiday now. We spend our holidays in places like Killarney and Wicklow, and in all fairness one would have to spend time in Dublin or one of the other big cities to find out.

The world is a much smaller place now than it was when I first moved to England, not to mention my parents' time - a journey that once took a week by sea is only a few hours on Concorde. When I first started taking my car to Ireland it was hoisted on board by crane - today I can drive on and off in a matter of minutes on some of the most modern car ferries in the world. Progress.

I still feel that the average British family would get far better value for their money if they were to holiday in Ireland, as opposed to sitting on crowded Spanish beaches, and suffering the inconvenience of French air strikes. There is also a certain element of British youngsters who bring disgrace on their country and blacken its name all over Europe and those same youngsters live a normal everyday life at home and never step out of line. They adopt an aggressive attitude towards people of other races, and they turn an international football game into World War three. They jeer and whistle during the playing of other countries' national anthems, something that never happens anywhere else that I know of. They seem to hate anyone who is not British. Thankfully they are a small minority and most British people are good honest folk and easy to get along with, and they get on well with the Irish.

On being Irish

Something I find very confusing is the cost of taking a car to Ireland. I just cannot for the life of me fathom out why it costs so much more to take a car to Ireland than to Europe, I know it is a longer journey but it also costs a lot more per mile. It is cheaper in low season to fly to Spain, and spend a week in a hotel than to take your car to Ireland. The ferries have improved an awful lot since the days of the old Princess Maud, when people were treated like cattle and jammed into confined spaces, this often after a long train journey and having to stand throughout - yes, today its much better. Something that is very obvious to the older traveller is that Irish people returning home don't seem to enjoy the sea journey as much as in the old days, even with much improved facilities. In the old days you were entertained throughout by accordion and fiddle music and a journey-long singsong. You never hear the laughter or witness the high spirits of the fifties. People seem more serious. This is probably due to the pressures and problems

175

people are facing today. There was no runaway inflation in the fifties and if a loaf of bread went up a penny there was an outcry. Today we have become accustomed to the inevitable price rises - where will it all end?

Every time I get off the boat in Dublin my mind goes back over the years to an August morning in the fifties, when I first sailed from my own shores, I feel the sadness I felt then and I am sure it is a feeling shared by the sons and daughters of Erin who are scattered throughout the globe, and I know that I will always feel the same. I have spent St Patrick's Day in Boston and it was a wonderful experience, it makes one proud to be Irish and to see the esteem in which our people are held all over the World. My adopted City of Manchester has also done us proud with its St Patrick's Day parade, and the City has its own Irish week. It is hard to believe that my wife and I are grandparents and I ask myself where have all the years gone. My advice to the young is live every day to the full, and enjoy every minute because youth is fleeting and can never be recalled. No one knows what the future holds, but I can truthfully say that I have lived a full and active life and enjoyed good health for which I thank God - something that money cannot buy.

Though I have had some downs in my life, I consider that I have had a more exciting life than most people have and I consider myself lucky to have so many friends. My wonderful family and friends now surround me - where would one be without them? Making friends is what life is all about and I can say with complete honesty that I have made many; it is nice to know that people care about you, as life would be very lonely without friends. Being outspoken about subjects dear to my heart is not always considered to be the easiest way to court friendships, but at least you know those you have made are genuine.

I always try to practise Brother Mcaulif's motto "To Thine Own Self Be True". I have always instilled in my three sons a great pride in their heritage, and it is something I will carry to my grave. When I get off the boat in dear old Dublin, I have a great feeling of belonging and that I am among my own. I am free to talk about any subject I choose in what is now thank God the freest country on earth, long may it remain so. I cannot find adequate words to describe the feeling I experience when I get behind the wheel of my car knowing that the open road is before me and some of the loveliest scenery in the world. There is a lot wrong with Ireland and we in exile are not slow to voice our opinions about it- however on the credit side it has an awful lot to offer. There is nothing incurably wrong with our country, and you cannot put right over night what took many centuries to put wrong. It must have a lot to offer the millions of tourists who come to visit our shores every year, as they keep coming back.

I feel a stranger in my hometown these days. So many of the people I care for are not there any more, and indeed some have gone to a better place I hope. Thady's house is now in decay with the roof falling in, and I get the most sad and nostalgic feeling when I drive past what remains of it. A new bypass has cut off the old road and all that I have left are my memories. If I had my life to live over again would I change anything? Some things perhaps. However I would not change the things that really matter. I would marry the same girl, I would box, play Gaelic football, rugby, soccer and golf. I would also make the same friends.

It is not always easy in a strange land to stand up for the ideals you were brought up to believe in, but I have always remained steadfast in my beliefs, and nothing or nobody could ever bring any influence to bear that would make me change them. I would be more cautious about some things I have done, and not place so much trust in some people - it can be painful to find out that they have more than one face. I am now close to completing my fiftieth year in exile and I have met some prejudice but in all honesty not a lot.

Your average Englishman likes a pint of beer, follows his local football team often fanatically, and some like to bet on the horses, and he has enough problems of his own without having to listen to the problems of others. He is mostly a fair minded man who does not care what is happening in Ireland or anywhere else for that matter, and most of those I have discussed Ireland's problems with would like to hand back our six counties tomorrow. They rightfully point out that it is a burden on the taxpayer, and they would gladly part with the problems they have had to face because of the colonising done by their ancestors. "It is a case of the evil that men do lives after them", and that I believe was written by an Englishman, something that a country boy like me would never have the wisdom to write. I feel that I must by now have exhausted my reader's patience, if he hasn't given up long before now. I will soon start my second fifty years on foreign soil, and if the second fifty is as exciting as I found the first I may put pen to paper at a future date. For now the well has run dry. So be it.

ISBN 141202084-0

9 781412 020848